BECOMING DANISH

BECOMING DANISH

JOHN CAMPBELL

Copyright © 2025 by John Campbell
All rights reserved. No part of this book may be reproduced in any manner whatsoever without written permission except in the case of brief quotations embodied in critical articles and reviews.
First Printing, 2025

ISBN (Paperback): 978-1-7638468-0-7
ISBN (eBook): 978-1-7638468-1-4

Cover design by Vicki Kersey

To my daughters, Jessica and Emily, who have lived most of their lives with the experience of youth exchange present. Thank you for being amazing host sisters to so many. More importantly, thank you for being the most incredible daughters a father could ever hope for. You both inspire me every day and I love you beyond description.

Contents

Dedication	v
Acknowledgements	viii
Preface	x
1 Am I The One?	1
2 First Impressions	7
3 Welcome To Aarhus	19
4 Family One	33
5 Euro Extravaganza	55
6 Family Two	93
7 The England Experience	107
8 Getting Together	119
9 Marvellous Marselisborg	135
10 Aarhus The City	161
11 Remembering Ry	175
12 Family Three	183
13 Christmas Traditions	197
14 A Final Farewell	207
Epilogue	215

Acknowledgements

This work is dedicated, with deepest gratitude, to the many people who made 1992 a reality for me. While I fear omissions and apologise for any, special mention must go to:

The Australians

Mum, Dad, Ellen, Karen, Mark, Darren and my extended family of grandparents, aunts, uncles and cousins for the love and support I carried with me always.

All the Rotarians at the Mermaid Beach Rotary Club and on the District 9640 Youth Exchange committee for preparing me (and my family) so very thoroughly and well, then trusting in, and supporting, me throughout.

Thanks to all of you. I know that while I was physically more than 15 000 kilometres away, your unconditional support and encouragement was always very near.

The Danes

Poul, Inge, Charlotte N, Vibeke, Marianne N, Per, Dorte, Ulrik, Rikke, Kaare, Christian, Grete, Charlotte K, Nicolai, Marianne K, Claus, Barbara, Martin, Lars, Phillip, Tina, Xenia for welcoming me so lovingly into not only your homes, but your hearts. You allowed me to so easily and quickly become your son, your brother and your friend.

The teachers, administrators and friends at Marselisborg Gymnasium for not only an outstanding education but an incredible cultural immersion. I always felt like I belonged and was accepted.

The Rotarians at the Aarhus Nordvestre Rotary Club for hosting me with such enthusiasm and kindness. I felt welcome at every club meeting and event – supported and safe.

The Exchange Students

Those who shared the extraordinary experiences of exchange with me and who simply understood the journey. So many of you were responsible for instilling wonderful memories in my mind and love in my heart.

I am so thankful that over 30 years later, my connection to nearly all of you – in each of these categories – is still as strong as it ever was. You are all incredible humans. While I would love everyone to know who you all are in my story, I have changed names in the book to protect and respect privacy.

I would also like to thank those who have been encouraging of this work, who have provided comment and guidance along the writing journey and who have motivated me to move from manuscript to published. Your support and encouragement are much appreciated, and I'll be forever grateful.

While you all have my appreciation, special mention must go to Vicki, who has been instrumental in making this book a reality.

Preface

I invite you to be a part of this exploration into the very spirit and essence of what being an exchange student was like in a very different time - 1992. I invite you to be reminded of the innocence of youth and the growth that occurs in all of us late in our tender teens, and I invite you to travel Europe through the pages of this book. Most importantly, I invite you to meet the wonderful people of Denmark, who took this Australian youth exchange student and defined his entire character with acceptance, interest and love.

Nothing about an exchange year is ordinary. The vast majority of exchange students will experience the extraordinary, but for a fortunate few, theirs will, quite simply, be beyond extraordinary... theirs will be 'wow!' It's been said that exchange is 'a year in a life and a life in a year', which speaks to living life in a very heightened way. Many aspects of teenage life unfold more intensely on exchange, especially if the opportunities presented are embraced fully. Knowing you only have one year requires a 'throw caution to the wind' approach and complete immersion.

An indisputable consequence of my contact with people of many nationalities was the exchange of ideas and experiences, which permitted me to gain a clear and profound vision of the human existence.

I have to share this story; I feel compelled to do so. I do not do justice to my families, both Australian and Danish, to Denmark, to Rotary, to my many Australian and Danish friends, or to myself by simply cherishing every memory I hold dear. Words are not enough, but they are all I have with which to fulfil this purpose. I am about to reveal the true experiences of a 'wow!' exchange and in doing so, open my heart and my soul, with all the unashamed passion and vigour with which I lived those experiences.

I humbly, but proudly, invite you to experience
"Becoming Danish".

1

Am I The One?

What would you do if we sent you to a country where you had to go to school in a cold, dark castle? What would you do if you were asked to sauna naked? These were just a couple of the questions asked of me in 1991 by the District panel in my quest to become a Rotary International Youth Exchange Student – to where, I had no idea.

No doubt the Rotarians asking those questions had heard all kinds of answers to them before, some rehearsed and some unrehearsed. I was confident that it was my answers to the questions about Australia and being Australian that were rather unique. Unique because I'd had the rare experience at the age of 11 of having travelled Australia, extensively and full-time, over a 13-month period with my family. Every state, both territories and within them, hundreds of wonderful cities and towns. Amazing landscapes, money-can't-buy adventures and, importantly, meeting a truly diverse mix of Australians ensured the experience was unique. That, in turn, gave me insights and perspectives with which to give elaborate, informed and unique answers during my interview.

I admit to being largely ignorant at the time about what Rotary Youth Exchange was but still managed to be selected for the program. I had stumbled into the process by virtue of a local lawyer named Peter, who was also a Rotarian. During a week of work experience in my school holidays, Peter took me to a Rotary meeting of his club. It just so happened that a girl, who had recently returned from Germany, was presenting her experiences to the club that had sponsored her exchange. Her story was truly extraordinary, and I was in awe. That much must have been obvious to Peter, who only days later rang to enquire whether I was interested in applying for youth exchange. Naturally, I jumped at the opportunity, a response he appeared to be expecting because he had already arranged for my interview with the relevant club members the next day.

Despite selection and despite having done my homework on what Rotary Youth Exchange was, time revealed to me that I had remained mostly ignorant of the honour that had been bestowed upon me. What I was acutely aware of, however, was that even though the District panel had selected me for exchange, I still had to prove myself by successfully completing my senior year of high school and by attending two briefing camps before embarking upon the journey of a lifetime.

The first of those briefing camps was in July 1991. It felt as though the weeks between selection and the camp didn't exist. I was grateful for the fact that time had been kind and had passed so quickly. My excitement was clearly hard to contain.

Together with my parents, we drove to Cedar Lake Country Club where we joined with the other selected exchange students, their parents, Rotarians and a number of newly returned exchange students. Our expectations were that the camp would inform and prepare us. As it turned out, the camp was an adventure in itself. Sure, it informed and prepared us but feverishly rehearsed ad-hoc performances by the students and no-holds-barred question and answer sessions meant that it also entertained us. We all basked in the light that shone from the eyes of those exchange students who had recently returned from their respective exchanges. Their extraordinary stories captured the attention of all present and held us captive until the next story was told. I knew at that point that my life was soon to change forever.

Briefing camp two was held in December 1991. One thing an exchange student learns early on, even as early as the briefing camps, is that every experience of exchange seems to somehow, without explanation, continue to amaze and astound you. You continue to learn and continue to grow. If the briefing camp at Tyalgum Tops Holiday Farm was a ride, we certainly got our money's worth. It is truly bizarre and remains an age-old phenomenon why we are so irreversibly drawn in life toward something we know little or nothing about. I knew of exchange that which I had been told, but I didn't really *know* what it was. This camp involved more formalities, as we were given itineraries and Rotary jackets. These blue jackets, lined and with a map of Australia embroidered on them, became a repository for all manner of souvenirs. My jacket quickly became adorned with badges, pins and even bottle-tops from every corner of the world. They were exchanged, as indeed I was about to be.

Soon after the last briefing camp, I received my congratulatory letter from the District Governor of Rotary for District 9640. I read, with exhilaration and excitement, the words of encouragement and praise authored for my benefit. As I reached the part that said, *...finally I say farewell*, I could sense the nervous tension tingle within my being. This was real, I was about to leave Australia and live the life of an exchange student in Denmark. I was about to leave all that I knew and loved, for something I didn't.

No departure of this magnitude happens without a bon voyage celebration. Although just another party, it is difficult to do my going-away party justice. It was the culmination of my twelve years of education, an early 18th birthday party and a send-off all rolled into one. Gathered around me were many of the reasons why leaving was so difficult. My parents and sisters, with whom I had an inseparable bond, and my many friends, some of whom I had known since early childhood, were all going to be missed terribly; without exception, though, they encouraged me to embrace the adventure.

While I knew that most of the goodbyes were temporary, I was forced to acknowledge that for some, it was forever. My faithful friend and beloved pet dog was aged and ill and despite a will to live greater than any I have known, I knew he would not be there to welcome me home. In his thirteen years of life, Joe had survived two disgraceful poisonings from neighbours, attack from ticks and, most damagingly, near death from heartworm. Yet, I knew it was the battle against the time of my exchange that he would lose. The other goodbye I feared might be permanent was to my girlfriend, Michelle. We had spoken of commitment, and I believed it would be possible. Sadly, my belief was shattered when I made the discovery of Michelle's secret solace found in another man. As difficult as it was, I looked to the positive side and recognised that the relationship was one less item of emotional baggage I had to take with me.

The first entry in my little black book – my 1992 diary – was made the day before my departure and reads, *It is now the day before I leave and my emotions are running riot.* No poignant, powerful prose there, but powerful proof of the true feelings of a seventeen-year-old youth about to leave behind all that he was and all that he knew for something and somewhere largely unknown. Wednesday, 8 January 1992 was really the first day of the rest of my life. It was the day I embarked upon my journey of discovery to the small Scandinavian land known as Denmark. I knew that day wasn't going to be easy, but I wasn't prepared for just how hard it was. I had quite the farewell entourage with Mum, Dad, my sister Karen, my grandmother who was visiting from Sydney, and my best friend Rob. We were punctual to the minute and arrived two hours before departure as instructed. It quickly became obvious that we were the only punctual ones, and that we had to resign ourselves to the fact that our flight was delayed for two hours. That meant that my emotions had to withstand four hours of torturous testing before I could finally say goodbye. I wasn't the only student departing Brisbane that day. There were several others, including Allan and Allison, both from my District and both also going to Denmark. We checked in together, although Allison had to unpack at check in to lighten her luggage. We had been warned about excess luggage and that students had been forced to unpack at the point of check in before. Admittedly, it is difficult to pack for an absence of one year.

I was not the only one embarking on air travel that day. I had to, prematurely and privately, farewell my mother, who was flying to Sydney to send-off my sister. Ellen was travelling with a school group to the United States of America. Had I not been selected for youth exchange, I would have been joining Ellen in America. Ellen and I had already said goodbye during the preceding week, and upon reflection, it was perhaps good practice for what was necessary at the Brisbane International Airport with the rest of my family. Mum and I did not shed any tears, but I could have easily allowed her heartfelt embrace to continue for hours. My mother was more precious to me than any gem and more valuable than any treasure, and to let go of her loving hold was one of the most difficult things I had ever done.

Then came the boarding call. It was something of a paradox because I was dreading the call but excited by it at the same time. The loudspeaker bellowed out the call for all passengers to board QF51 and, that instant, my first stage of growth and learning occurred. I had to reach deep – very, very deep and find the strength to take those tentative steps through the boarding gate onto the tarmac. I could have still changed my mind, still turned back to the ones I loved and knew would welcome me home. Instead, I wiped the tears that had welled in my eyes and bravely embraced my father, my grandmother, my youngest sister and my best friend. I whispered private words to each of them and stepped though the doorway. It had always amused me how on-lookers naively wave at the plane on a tarmac in which their loved ones sit, thinking they could see them. However, it was I who was naive, as it become obvious to me that I could see my relatives and friends waving from the viewing enclosure. Yet another lesson learned.

This was not my first flight but was certainly unlike any trip I had taken. Not only were my senses heightened by what had just transpired inside the airport, but also the sheer size of the aeroplane was unfamiliar to me. I had not been on such an aircraft before. Rows upon rows of seats, more than a single aisle, and big screens for movie viewing were the noticeable features. Another feature that appealed to me was not known until just before we lifted off. The power and thrust of the plane seemed far superior to that which I had experienced before.

It wasn't very long before the head flight attendant introduced herself to us. Perhaps, as students, we were to receive special treatment. Alice was a lovely lady, with short brown hair, a small fringe and a gorgeous wide smile. Later in the flight, I spoke with Alice and asked whether it might be possible to visit the cockpit, which I did in her presence. The Captain generously let me wear his cap, embroidered as it was with the Australian coat-of-arms positioned just above a big red 'Q' for Qantas, and gold wings. A thick band of woven gold silk separated the top of the cap from the brim, and it fitted rather well. It didn't fit well enough to let me touch the controls though, not even for a moment. I was permitted a photo wearing the cap and sitting with Alice in the spare seat in the cockpit. It seemed the Captain could take photos and fly the plane at the same time.

The speed of the plane was only outpaced by the emotions that were racing throughout my body and mind. I knew it was too late to turn back, but I didn't have the same conviction about the decision I had made to leave. I was excited but afraid, nervous but eager, and trusted that I would soon know whether or not the decision was the correct one. I would have to wait 24 hours before I could start to make that assessment.

2

First Impressions

Exhausted, but at the very same time excited, I arrived at Copenhagen International Airport ready to transfer to my last flight for many months. Aboard the flight from Singapore to Copenhagen, all the exchange students from Australia met, bonded and befriended each other with astonishing speed and genuineness. Despite only hours earlier being completely unknown to each other, we all faced the same challenges and opportunities that would change us all forever. In exactly the time it took us to fly from Singapore to Copenhagen, we went from being strangers to being friends.

Disembarking from the plane at Copenhagen didn't expose us to the Danish winter. Instead, it led us directly into the customs area and, eventually, into the greater part of the main terminal. Given the Danish reliance on central heating, we noticed little, if any, change in the temperature in the airport. There is strength in numbers, and we were all grateful for the fact that while none of us could read the signs or understand the calls over the loudspeaker, as a group, we could still communicate in our mother tongue. We remained a group as we walked towards the front doors of the terminal to where a waiting bus would transfer us to the domestic air terminal. We had one more flight – a further 30 minutes – to a city called Odense. Between the airport exit and the doors of the bus, we were exposed to the weather and exposed in a big way. I, for one, had never experienced such a cold. I had seen and enjoyed the Australian snow at Falls Creek but not with the penetrating bite of chilling cold. Three metres seemed a significant distance as we all huddled together in search of the front doors of the waiting bus. To our unanimous delight, the bus too was heated, and we all thawed out just in time to disembark and board our final flight.

My first real contact with the Danish population was intensive and continuous for the entire length of the flight to Odense, which is the largest city on the Danish island of Fyn. Her name was Christina, and she worked for the Danish Department of Natural Resources. Given the seating arrangements on the plane, I was separated from the other exchange students and was alone with an attractive lady who I guessed to be in her early 30s. I have never been comfortable with the term 'typical' when describing individuals, but to the extent people typically relate blonde hair and blue eyes to the Scandinavians, then my travel companion was typically Danish. Luckily for me, her command of the English language was far superior to my knowledge of Danish. I learned that Christina was travelling to Odense to deliver a presentation to local high schools on contemporary issues regarding the Danish environment. Christina learned that I was an Australian exchange student with Rotary who was travelling to Odense to participate in an intensive three-week language course before moving to my new home of Aarhus on Denmark's mainland.

I gave Christina one of the many Qantas stickpins I had collected on my flight from Brisbane to Singapore, with the Aussie kangaroo its main feature. I discovered for the first of many times, the joyous response that such an apparently simple expression of international kindness can produce. This was truly something special.

Having had the delightful travel partner that I did, the half-hour flight passed quickly. As I approached the landing above the stairs to the plane, I realised Odense was no mammoth metropolis. There was a small terminal in the distance and many metres of tarmac to cross before again feeling the warmth of central heating. We all spared no time in carving a path through the thick fog and mist that so entirely engulfed us as we made our way to the terminal doors. Inside was an ocean of Danish people there to meet and greet us and welcome us into their homes and hearts. My excitement started to wane a little when my name was the only one not on any of the small placards being hoisted high into the air by the many host parents who had arrived to take us to our temporary homes. It was only moments later, however, that Bo walked through the terminal to introduce himself as my first host father.

A tall, bearded man, Bo's presence immediately comforted me as together we collected my luggage that had successfully followed me from the airports in Brisbane, Singapore and Copenhagen. Bo had a deep, calming voice, but I sensed a hint of nervousness within it as was within mine. Bo had not met an Australian before, and here he was welcoming one into his home, his family, his life. At that time, the true meaning of exchange started to emerge from my young and underdeveloped understanding of the term. Bo and I were nervous, because we were about to learn from each other, about to experience something we had not experienced before. Admittedly, my experiences were more pronounced, given that I was the foreigner, and I was so overwhelmed by my surroundings.

Apart from the obvious differences that were so undeniably present, such as the bitterly cold weather, there were other less obvious differences that greeted me as I started the process of assimilation. Bo escorted me through the blanket of fog and cold toward his white Mazda 626. Having loaded my luggage into the boot of the car, I made my way to the passenger side of the vehicle. Bo's amused expression suggested to me that I had done something funny, and it wasn't until I opened the door to find a steering wheel that I realised what it was. It was not a difficult concept to grasp but again one that was not immediately familiar to me. The Danes, along with the greater population of Europe, drive on the right-hand side of the road and thus their cars are left-hand drive. Having come to this realisation didn't make it any easier on me as we travelled those first few kilometres from the airport toward Bo's home on Stockfletsvej in Odense West. The trip was not uncomfortable as much as it was different.

About 25 minutes later, we arrived at Bo's home. The house was an older home and quite typical of the architecture of the time. It had a high-pitched roof, frosted with just a hint of pale snow covering its extremities. Earthy red-brown bricks had been used as the external cladding on the three-storey construction. A glass enclosure formed the entrance to the home and was misted from the warmth of the air inside. We unloaded my luggage and went into the house. Apart from Bo, the first of the family to greet me was the family's pet dog, Chicko. A truly delightful dog with a thick and fluffy coat that quite obviously provided adequate protection from the elements outside. It has been said that dogs speak all languages and that certainly appeared true enough for Chicko. I prefer to think that all pets simply respond well to love and respect – wherever they may live. Whatever the explanation, I enjoyed spending time with Chicko and his ever-appreciative look and wagging tail suggested to me that the feeling was mutual. One thing that was becoming more and more obvious with the passing of every minute, was that Denmark was serving up a banquet of first impressions every time my senses were introduced to something new. At the time, I was hardly able to pass judgement about whether this was a typical Danish residence, but it turned out it was. The cottage style windows with white timber framing, the low hanging lights and of course the central heating units throughout are common to many Danish homes. The feature I found most common to every Danish home I had the privilege of visiting was the warm, homely atmosphere. The kind, caring and genuinely welcoming nature of the Danish folk, mixed so perfectly with the very air that was warmed by the central heating, meant I felt at home with every visit. Having just travelled some 24 hours, my senses had every right to be dulled, tired and incapable of receiving such wondrous experiences, but they weren't. It was as though I had simply stepped through some imaginary door from the Queensland summer to the Odense winter and I could formulate no explanation for why this was so. After sharing a few moments over coffee, Bo showed me to my bedroom and invited me to get some rest, as he had to leave and return to some pressing matters at work. He told me that my host mother Astrid and host sister Freja would be home within a couple of hours.

The minute my head touched the pillow, my eyelids came crashing down and I fell into the deepest sleep I'd had for many nights. In fact, it was the only sleep I'd had since leaving Australia. Some four hours later I woke to the sounds of footsteps above. Initially I felt displaced, a little disorientated. My bedroom was on the ground floor; above it were two floors of living and bedroom space. A few steps along the hallway, from which my bedroom was accessed, was the laundry. I splashed some icy water over my face, fixed my hair and decided to venture upstairs to meet the owners of the footsteps I had heard. Freja was the only one home at that time, and we made our tentative self-introductions. Freja was a thin 20-year-old girl with curly blonde hair and kind eyes set behind thin-framed spectacles. Despite the obvious impediment of language, we were able to converse with consummate ease. It only became apparent upon reflection, that communication is far more than simply language with its various words and phrases but is something more intangible. Freja and I were able to put each other at ease despite not knowing exactly the words to say. It was not long before Astrid, my host mother, arrived home from work. Astrid was quiet, almost shy in the beginning, but it was clear to me that behind the shyness, she was as excited to have me there as I was to be there. Astrid and Bo had three children, all girls and only Freja lived at home. Ida, the eldest, was a university student studying Theology, and Josefine, the youngest, was a student at a boarding college. Both Ida and Josephine lived in Aarhus, which by coincidence was my ultimate destination after completing language school in Odense. It would only be a few days, though, before I had the pleasure of meeting them.

I was the only exchange student in the group who got to enjoy some travel during the short time in Odense. My host parents took me to visit Aarhus during my stay with them. They saw it as a good opportunity to not only show me my permanent 'hometown', but also to visit with their other two daughters, Ida and Josefine. We went to dinner and ate at a great, but expensive, restaurant called Den Viking Bøfhus (The Viking Steakhouse). It was the site of one of my most embarrassing moments. Bo had bought a lovely bottle of red wine and as we charged our glasses, he said, "Skål." This sounded very much like the Aussie slang word skull, so I drank the full glass from start to finish. The horrified look on the faces of my host family signalled immediately that I'd suffered a communication breakdown. The Danish word Skål actually means cheers and another lesson was learned.

Language school was challenging for most but easier for some. I can't pretend I was one of the few who had little trouble in grasping what many believe is one of the hardest languages to learn. The school itself was within a technical college about ten minutes bicycle ride from my host home, although in sub-zero temperatures, it seemed much longer. We had different teachers in the morning and afternoon, with the morning teacher being far better in my opinion. I suppose, in retrospect, it may have been because the afternoon teacher thought I was enjoying myself too much to be giving serious enough attention to the course. This was true and false all in one. I was enjoying myself, but I wasn't neglecting the course.

All the Australian and New Zealand exchange students were placed into one of two classes, but the rooms were side-by-side, closed off by a retractable wall. Within each classroom, we were seated in workshop-style seating, all facing each other, rather than the traditional rows of seats and desks. All the lessons were hard, but on exchange, as with life, some lessons are harder learned than others.

Day nine of language school and I found myself learning a lesson the hard way. This was not a lesson in the classroom but within the school grounds. Just off the road that ran through the school was a pond, which was iced over from the preceding days of sub-zero temperatures. Being unfamiliar with the art of reading the ice and being adventurous, I made my way out onto the frozen pond where I slipped and slid over its glassy surface. I was ice skating, only without the skates. I had ignored warnings from some Danish students who attended the school that the ice was not thick enough to hold me, because I had seen others on it the day before. So out I went to enjoy myself. Sure enough, the ice held, and I was having a great time. Then a few other exchange students came out to join me. We were standing about ten paces from the edge of the pond when we heard it start to creak and crack below us. It was similar to the sound made when liquid is poured onto ice cubes fresh from a freezer, only many times louder. We determined it was necessary to get off the ice immediately and began to slip and slide toward the safety of land. I was still two metres from the edge when the ice finally gave way, and I went splashing into the icy depths below. Luckily for me, those icy depths were actually only about waist deep and I was able to clamber to the edge. I was frightfully cold and in need of a change of clothes, so I made my way home, embarrassed by the knowledge that I'd learned a lesson the hard way – listen to the locals!

I was the first of the exchange students to turn eighteen while on exchange and actually the first, by only by a few days, to have a birthday that year. I was very fortunate that I arrived in Denmark four days before my 18th birthday. A day later, and I would have been ineligible for exchange to that country. Any thoughts I may have had about feeling lonely on what, for many Australians, is a special birthday, were quickly and utterly dispelled upon joining my host family for breakfast. Scattered all throughout the room were tiny Danish flags and flying high on the flagpole in the back yard was yet another flag.

Without wishing to sound repetitious, that morning I made yet another discovery about my new homeland and its people. Danes are a very proud people, and they acknowledge special occasions such as birthdays by raising the Danish flag and placing smaller ones around their homes. I was truly overwhelmed by the limitless hospitality of my host family and yet there was more to come. My host parents gave me a wonderful book and presented me with a birthday card and another book that had been sent by my first permanent host family further to the north. I was asked whether I would like to invite a friend for dinner that night and, at that time, the student living closest to me was Kristina. I had met Kristina on the plane from Brisbane to Singapore and discovered that she was from a rural town in central Queensland. Kristina was only too happy to join us and walked over at about 5:30pm. My host mother had toiled in the kitchen and, in addition to a delightful dinner, had baked me a Kagemand which we all enjoyed later that evening. A Kagemand was a cake shaped like a person and the birthday boy got to cut off the head. I retired to my bedroom that night trying to grapple with just how kind these people were. I had been a part of their lives for less than a week, and they were indulging me. This went well beyond obligation – it was genuine kindness.

The smooth, rounded and well-worn cobblestones of the dimly lit alley were shining from the melting snow as we made our way to Casa O'Dina. It was a quaint but expensive cafe in the heart of Odense. Having shared coffee, stories from the first week of language school and plenty of laughter, some of the more intrepid of us then made our way to The Rocks nightclub in search of Danish nightlife. Most of us had seen the inside of a nightclub at some stage in our lives but not a Danish one and not together as a group of Australians. This automatically made us somewhat of an attraction. Most of us were accompanied by siblings from our host families or by Danish friends we had made during our short stay. I met a most attractive girl named Emma, who was also on exchange from Australia. More specifically, she was from a north-eastern suburb of Melbourne in the state of Victoria. I found it remarkable during those early days in Odense that not only was I meeting wonderful Danish people but also meeting people from all over my own country, whom I would otherwise never have met. Emma and I felt so comfortable with each other and exchanged the sad stories of the failure of our respective relationships left behind. The emotion was so intense and all consuming. It seemed so sudden, but Emma and I found ourselves lost in the passionate embrace of each other, and before too long, we had spent over an hour together. It didn't take too long for our better judgment to kick in and we decided not to proceed further. We both realised that we had twelve months ahead of us and we did not want to complicate those months with a teenage relationship. Of course, logistically, such a relationship would have been difficult anyway, given we were soon to move to different parts of the country. Remaining good friends was the sensible thing to do and something we both hoped would be our reality. I also had the pleasure of the company of both my host sister, Freja and our neighbour, Nora. Together, we enjoyed ourselves at the nightclub until the hour was late and it was time to go home. As we arrived home, Nora asked that I join her in her house for a hot chocolate. As with many of the mores of Denmark, I was unaware at that time of the acceptability of such an invitation. I didn't want to get off on the wrong foot, so to speak, and was therefore reassured by Freja's approval of the invitation. I joined Nora next door and after making the hot chocolate in her kitchen, we made our way to her bedroom. We listened to soft music, talked and enjoyed our beverages.

As it was with my initial introductions with my host family, certain human interactions seem not to be bound by language or culture but something more intrinsic. With Nora, it was an undeniable attraction fuelled by adolescent emotion. Nora was as tentative as I was about the situation we found ourselves in, but she was the one to find the courage to define the moment. We were soon sharing much more than chocolate and, in a sense, making our own music. However, certain undeniable truths started flooding to the foremost of my thoughts. Highest of these truths were the Rotary rules for exchange students and the fact that I was leaving Odense within a fortnight. Coupled with the high morals my parents had instilled in me, these thoughts brought to a prompt end the course on which we were headed. We decided our new-found friendship was paramount, and I wished her goodnight and returned home, her virginity retained and my integrity intact.

As a group, all the exchange students were treated to a comprehensive tour of Odense. We attended the Odense Council, and we all found a seat around the great oval shaped chamber in which the Council representatives met. The timber used throughout was a type of pine or beech and the workmanship was superb. We were educated about the method of local government in Odense and of the history of the City, which dated back more than a thousand years. Of course, no tour of Odense is complete without a visit to what was once the very cramped home of Hans Christian Andersen. The famous Danish author of fairy tales lived in the house until 1819.

An exchange student learns very quickly to be much more than simply a student. In fact, most exchange students, during the course of their exchange, take on such roles as diplomat, tourist, ambassador, photographer, counsellor and entertainer. This latter role was something that didn't come naturally to me, although the experience was an enjoyable one. We had only just started to feel comfortable in our new surrounds when we realised that our wonderful time in Odense was approaching its end. It was incumbent upon us to thank our various hosting Rotary Clubs, and this was traditionally done at the regular weekly meeting of the Clubs. My Club, the Odense Vestre Rotary Klub, had its weekly meetings every Monday evening and had made us all feel extremely welcome. I had, in the short time I was there, developed a close friendship with a fellow exchange student named Matthew, from Orange in New South Wales. His early command of the new language was far superior to mine and he was often a great help to me when I met with difficulty. Matthew and I performed lip-sync to *Old Time Rock & Roll* as we made our entrance by sliding on our knees across the polished timber floor. We were wearing our prized Rotary jackets and dark sunglasses. We were received with much applause and adulation, which made the subsequent bruises on our knees worth it. Later, Matthew and I joined a few others to perform Billy Joel's great hit, *For the Longest Time* in a capella style. However, we too were entertained by our hosts as they fed us a lovely dinner and showed us a film on Odense.

The remaining four days of language school were also the last four days I was to spend in the most hospitable and memorable Danish community of Odense. On the final evening in Odense, Rotary arranged a farewell party for all the exchange students. It was relatively sedate but an important event on the calendar. We all exchanged contact cards and best wishes and made our way home to enjoy our final evening with our host families.

Our contact cards became critical in developing our network of national and international exchange friendships. Each Rotary District had different styles and kinds of contact cards, some single sided and in basic black and white, others in colour. Far more elaborate were those from my District. The card folded in two, resulting in four business card sized surfaces, with a photograph, map, District information, address and provision for making notes all on the one card. But the type of card didn't matter, the information on it did.

The next morning, I was up early to catch the train that would take me to my final destination of Aarhus. Saying goodbye to my host family resembled having to say goodbye to my own family seventeen days earlier. Admittedly it wasn't quite as difficult, but nonetheless emotional. How that was possible, I had no idea. No amount of rationalising made it any easier. In the end, I resigned myself to the fact that the level of emotion was directly linked to the level of affection I had developed with my host family. On reflection, it was the first of many examples of emotional connections being made in what might seem impossibly short amounts of time. Exchange time is simply more intense. For that I was grateful, not sad. I assured my delightful host family that I would visit again before returning to Australia. With that solemn vow and with plenty of hugs and kisses, I boarded the train and took my allocated seat.

3

Welcome To Aarhus

Aarhus is Denmark's second largest city and is home to many wonderful people and places. It is approximately 180 kilometres from the Danish/German border and 230 kilometres from the northern most tip of the Danish mainland. It is located on the east of mainland Denmark and is a harbour city. While there is evidence to suggest the first city wall was dated around the year 934, the first City Charter dates back to 1449. Given the city was settled so long ago, it is rich in history, and there is much evidence of that. It is, however, a very cosmopolitan city, rich in modern culture, art and sport. It boasts beautiful landscapes, including the beech forests along the Marselisborg coastline and the Queen's summer palace with its expansive park grounds.

Train travel itself was not entirely unfamiliar to me as I had ridden trains at home. However, the Aarhus train station was unlike anything I had visited before. Despite having just travelled two hours on a modern example of train engineering, the platform and station were things from a time long passed. As the train eased into the Aarhus station, I again felt the uneasy, nervous tension I had felt when landing in Odense. My arrival in Aarhus, however, was a much grander affair than in Odense. My first, and third, host families were there, so too was my counsellor and the President of the Aarhus Nordvestre Rotary

Klub. I was overwhelmed by such a welcome but most grateful at the same time.

I said goodbye to my welcoming committee and joined my first host family for the 30-minute drive back to their home in Brabrand, a suburb to the north of Aarhus. I had recognised my host family from the photographs they had sent to me when I was still at home in Australia. My host father, Bendt, was a Professor of History at the Aarhus University and was a tall, well-spoken Dane with whom I quickly developed an inseparable bond. My host mother, Clara, was a reference librarian at the Aarhus City Library and was as sweet and caring a lady as I had ever met. Her incomparable commitment to making me welcome and a part of her family was something truly astounding. Then last but certainly not least, there was Erik. I did have two host brothers, however, Rasmus was, at that time, on exchange in the United States of America. Erik had experienced exchange at the University level, also in America. He was tall like his father, but his mother's features could readily be identified in him. Erik was a student at the Aarhus University and was well into his Political Science Degree when I joined the family. I felt immediately at ease with Erik, although he was my senior by about four years. I knew at that very early stage, that with Erik, I would have a brother for life.

The family was complemented by its pet dog, Vanja, a six-year-old female German shepherd. She was as eager to greet me as my host family had been and jumped all over me from the start. Their house was a comfortable two-storey residence and while markedly different in architecture, was similar inside to that of my host family's home in Odense. As with every Danish residence, there was the obvious feature of central heating units throughout and again, low hanging lights in the dining, living and lounge rooms. A feature unique to Bendt and Clara's home, however, was the noticeable presence of books from all nature of literature, which were not only well organised, but catalogued for ease of reference.

After I unpacked my belongings, Bendt and Clara invited me on a walk along Brabrand Sø, which was a large, but generally shallow lake, which weaved its way from Brabrand into and through the city to the harbour. It was a haven for wildlife, especially many species of birds, and there were bird viewing enclosures set at strategic positions around the lake. Not that I ever walked it, but there was also a path constructed in 1956 that stretched from near my host family's house to the centre of Aarhus. In the other direction, it was possible to take paths to the nearby towns of Skanderborg and Ry. I would later visit both those towns but always by bus or train.

On our return, we sat down to a lovely lunch of rye bread, cold meats and condiments, and Carlsberg beer. I had enjoyed sandwiches made on Danish rye bread before, but these were cut from loaves home-made by Clara, to an old family recipe. They were absolutely delicious. Of course, even apart from the type of bread, sandwiches in Denmark were not like sandwiches at home. They are made on fairly narrow rectangles of rye bread with the filling placed on top. But the sandwich remains open in that no top piece of bread is applied. A popular ingredient on Danish rye bread sandwiches is leverpostej. Translated, this means liver paste and while available commercially, Clara also made her own leverpostej. That, too, was delicious. I was told it was very much an acquired taste and that many students never got the taste for eating it. But I took to it like a duck to water, especially when beetroot and fried onion was added to the sandwich.

The effects of the 2-hour train trip to Aarhus hardly compared to those following the 24 hours of air travel getting to Denmark, and I was quite willing to accept my host parents' invitation of a tour of Aarhus. We visited Marselisborg Gymnasium which was to be my new school in a few days' time and walked through the heart of the city. Proudly standing in that heart was the city's largest church which boasted the longest centre aisle in greater Europe. Called Domkirke, the church aisle was 93 metres long and seated around 1200 people. Its architecture seemed ancient, and its copper-based features were greening with tarnish and age. While certainly not ancient, the church had its origins dating back to around the year 1200. However, a fire in 1330 saw it virtually abandoned until around 1449, and then it was further damaged in 1642 when lightning struck the tower and destroyed some of the historic bells. Final works to the building were completed in 1931 and remained in that condition when I visited with Clara and Bendt. Two enormous solid timber doors, intricately carved by obviously patient and skilled craftsmen, secured the front entrance to the church. I had never before had to exert so much energy into the simple task of opening a door. No doubt the elaborate heavy iron work featured on the doors added to their weight. Equally impressive was the decorative brickwork framing the entrance doors. Adjacent to the church was a statue of King Christian X atop his Royal mount. It, too, had weathered the effects of age and environment, not to mention the presence of bird droppings. These two landmarks proved most useful to me in my early familiarisation with the city. There was so much to take in, and I had to remind myself that I had plenty of time to experience it all. Of course, with Bendt being a Professor of History and clearly having pride in his city, I was fortunate to get the added benefit of his knowledge of the city and the history of its buildings such as Domkirke.

Clara and Bendt certainly left no stone unturned when it came to welcoming me into their home. A few days after I arrived, they invited many of the neighbours in the street for a welcome dinner so that they could meet me. The neighbours were also very warm and welcoming, and I developed close friendships with several of them. Perhaps the biggest adaptation I had to make in my life was the way in which I dealt with my new-found popularity. I was never short of invitations to visit places, meet people and experience events of all kinds. My first invitation was from Erik who was joining some friends that evening at a party nearby. I was keen to meet Erik's friends and spend time with him, so readily accepted his invitation. Upon arriving at the party at Christian's house, I was immediately confronted with a conflict of principles. I had, many months prior, agreed to abide by the Rotary Rules which are often called the Four D's. 'No Drinking, No Driving, No Dating, No Drugs' as the saying went, was a simple statement encompassing the majority of the Rotary Rules. It goes without saying that these general rules were designed not to curb youthful exuberance and development but rather to guide an exchange student when faced with choices that could well have wide-ranging ramifications. Fortunately for our cohort, the Chairman of Rotary Youth Exchange in Denmark had told us in Odense that we should use our own discretion when faced with some of these tests. It was no wonder that he quickly and affectionately became known as Onkel Arnie – the world's funkiest Onkel. Onkel is the Danish word for Uncle and indeed many Rotarians also felt like family. In terms of the rules though, Onkel Arnie did go further to clarify that there was no scope for discretion on drugs and driving and both would be send-home offences. The discretion would, in other words, only apply to the rules about drinking and dating. While this advice was at odds with what I had been told at home, I figured the local rules would take precedence over the home rules. I therefore determined that I should not be a bore and chose to participate in the drinking games and festivities that were unfolding before me. I learned very early on, probably as early as that party, that many of the younger Danes were partial to a good time and enjoyed a drink or two. The important thing, however, was that the good time did not depend on the existence of alcohol but on the company of friends. I knew from the experience of my own close friendships that it often takes time to develop those relationships to that level. On exchange, everything is different. It took no time at all for me to become good friends with all present at the party and history has shown me that those friendships are lasting. I suppose that with the knowledge I only had twelve months in which to enjoy those newfound friendships, there was no time to waste. In the minds of my great Danish friends, this too was the case.

The next morning, my head was well aware of what I had done the evening before. It was not so much the memory, as it was the headache, that reminded me of the fun I had experienced at Christian's house. The legacy of the party would not encumber me, however, and I joined the family in the dining room for a lovely breakfast. My stomach was delighted to receive such fresh, tasty and less notorious ingredients than it had at the party the night before. The bread rolls, toasted golden brown, were just the place to spread layers of sweet jam or honey and the freshly squeezed orange juice perfectly complemented the food. The day had been dedicated to introducing myself to my new host family. Sure, they had already seen my application form and photographs but that was only indicative. I hauled out my photograph albums with my family and friends portrayed in them, and books about the Gold Coast. We discussed the Gold Coast, its people and attractions and how it was my birthplace. It was not long before discussion turned to the rest of Australia and my knowledge of it. Hindsight is a wonderful thing and when looking back, it was clear that many Danes, and many Europeans, were quite unaware of the sheer size of Australia. At least, if known, it was still surprising to most when put into comparative terms. When I would tell host families, friends, teachers and Rotarians that my home state alone was approximately 35 times larger in land mass than Denmark, or that Australia's largest single cattle property had a land mass about half the size of Denmark, there was often disbelief.

Unlike the other exchange students and unlike a lot of Australians, I had been fortunate enough in my youth to have travelled extensively around Australia. I explained how my parents had sacrificed to buy a bus and convert it to a motor home and embark on 13 months travelling our wonderful country. My host family could see from the passion and vigour with which I described the many experiences of those 13 months, that I had lost nothing by way of education in not attending school for that time. The inherent genuineness of my reflections on Australia appeared to be most gratefully received and enjoyed. The smiles on their faces, and on mine, indicated to me just how powerful the exchange of information could be and how universal this world of ours really is. It also highlighted that exchange is very much about mutual learning.

The weekend passed ever so quickly and my first day at school arrived. It was truly a strange feeling having a first day at school, given that a couple of months earlier, I had graduated from high school. This first day of school in Denmark was much like my first ever day at school in Australia many years earlier. Although I was much older and wiser, saying goodbye to my host family as they dropped me at school was difficult. My host family was my comfort zone, my safety net in new and unfamiliar surroundings. Fortunately for me, I was not the only Aussie starting school that day. Susan, an exchange student from Melbourne, was also lucky enough to be placed in Aarhus and at Marselisborg Gymnasium. The same Rotary Club that was hosting my exchange was also hosting Susan. As a result, we both shared the same counsellor in Sven who was present at the school for our first day. I had met Sven previously, although it was a very brief encounter upon my arrival in Aarhus. He was a large jovial man but clearly committed to ensuring that Susan and I were comfortable at all times. He was responsible for our introduction to the Principal of the school and to the school's counsellor. Having made the necessary introductions, Sven bid us farewell and left us in the welcoming hands of the Principal. Such was Sven's commitment, however, that only about two weeks later, he invited Susan and me to his house for a most glorious dinner. At dinner, we talked about our first impressions and any issues that had arisen either in our homes or at school. For me, there were no issues to discuss. Sven reconfirmed that he would always be available should we wish to speak to him about anything during our exchange. It really was comforting to know we had that support.

Of course, Sven could not be with us every day at school, so it was time to experience Marselisborg Gymnasium for the first time. An immediate and striking feature of the school was that the Principal, teachers and support staff were all addressed by their first names. This was an enormous adjustment for a student who had always addressed teachers by their surnames, sir or miss. An even greater and more striking feature revealed itself as we walked the halls of the school. Amidst clouds of smoke, the students were quite openly smoking cigarettes in front of and, in some cases, together with their teachers. This behaviour in Australian schools would see certain punishment, perhaps even suspension from school, while a teacher would more than likely be dismissed from service.

Founded in the late 1800s, the school itself was housed essentially in one large building. It was an old four-storey building with rather wide stairwells at either end. As the student population had grown over the years, the schoolhouse experienced extensions and additions, which caused it to have a mix and match type of finish. There was one smaller building detached from the main building, but it only housed two or three classrooms and was not often used. It was certainly a new experience being able to start and finish an entire school day without the need to walk outside. This was a welcome feature during winter!

Danish high school students were, from my experience, very close. In part, this was because, generally, the cohort would remain together throughout the three years of high school. They engaged in class parties where one student in the class would host a party for the rest of the class. They each took turns in doing this and the friendships between them were just extraordinary. It is for this reason that their ready acceptance of me was so worthy of my praise and gratitude. In particular, Hanne and Alexander both offered me every assistance from the very beginning. Hanne and Alexander appeared to be rather popular within not only the class but also the broader school community. Alexander was of medium height and build with black hair and a contagious sense of humour. Simply put, Hanne was beautiful. She was beautiful in every sense of the word. Hanne had an attractive face, highlighted by a mesmerising smile and big brown eyes in which young men could get lost for hours. She was kind beyond description and often went out of her way for my benefit.

It was not long before I was invited to my first class party at Jacob's house. I bought myself six Tuborg beers and departed my host family's home for Jacob's place. I was already familiar with some of the drinking games being played, and I settled in immediately to the social scene that unfolded before me. The hours quickly disappeared, as did Hanne's sobriety, and the class telephoned a taxi to take Hanne home. Despite Hanne's house being in the city and my host family's house being to the west, I suggested that I share the ride and see to it that Hanne arrived home safely. Although nothing was said, I was acutely aware that many of my classmates were questioning my motives, but they were nothing but honourable. During the drive into the city, it became obvious that my honour was to be tested. I had never before been the target of such a beautiful woman's affection, albeit from clouded judgment. I was cuddling her for comfort only and as she started to kiss my fingers and hands, I realised that much advantage could be taken in the circumstances. However, it was obvious that such an indiscretion on my part would cause intolerable tension with the rest of my class, not to mention the loss of respect I would suffer from my already dear friend, Hanne. Once in the city, I paid the taxi driver and asked him to wait for me to return in a few minutes. I then assisted Hanne up the several flights of stairs to the unit she shared with her mother. It is said that first impressions count, and I had not met Hanne's mother before. As Hanne was making considerable noise rummaging for her keys to the unit, her mother opened the door to see her daughter with some male that she had never met before. If first impressions count, then her initial impressions of me must have been poor, particularly when I couldn't understand any of her questions asked in rapid succession. I managed to call upon the little Danish I had mastered and introduced myself by name and that I was an exchange student from Australia. Any early apprehension on her part was immediately allayed by my chivalrous actions toward her daughter and she thanked me before taking Hanne inside. I was confident that, in context, the first impression was rather positive. I made my way back down the dimly lit staircase to the street outside. To my great dismay, the taxi had not waited as I had requested. It was very late, very cold and I had no idea where I was. There was nobody around for me to ask directions from and no change in my pockets for a telephone call, assuming of course that I could have found a public phone. For the first time on exchange, I felt very lost, very alone and actually a little scared. I wandered aimlessly for about 15 minutes and happened upon King Christian's statue in the city. I felt about as stiff as the statue of King Christian, as the cold had been relentless in its penetration of my clothing. However, I knew that just adjacent to the familiar landmark was a taxi bay and with that, I found a taxi and finally found my way home.

The results of my somewhat chivalrous actions were seen immediately the next week at school. It turned out that Eva, one of Hanne's closest friends, had called her early the next morning to see how she was but was only able to speak with Hanne's mother. My conduct was apparently the topic of conversation and Hanne's mother was very complimentary about my actions. Fortunately for me, this positive feedback filtered throughout the rest of the class, and I was from that point on, not only well liked, but also universally respected. Hanne too was most thankful and in one adventurous evening, I had earned her respect, admiration and importantly, very special friendship.

It was not all fun and games at Marselisborg Gymnasium. My new-found Danish friends had their high schooling to complete and while I had completed my high school education, it was necessary for me to continue to learn. I was having my horizons broadened, my tastes exposed to new flavours and my vocabulary expanded by an entirely new language. In fact, what I was doing every day of my Danish life was learning. I soon discovered that learning was not something you necessarily did with textbooks, teachers and classrooms. There was something more innate about learning, something intangible and difficult to describe. Sometimes it would happen consciously, other times many valuable lessons were learned without even realising it at the time. The classroom education was really one of the conscious learning experiences and was the venue of my first presentation to my class. It was Friday, 31 January 1992 and my class had arrived for Geography. In the Geography lesson the day before, our teacher had displayed maps of Australia and used them to point out where I was from and to teach the students the state capital cities. The class had chanted, "John, John, John" as they wanted me to talk with them on the subject. I suggested I take the class on Friday as it would allow me to prepare a more interesting presentation. I had wisely gathered a lot of information in many different forms before embarking on exchange. I had a video from my local council, colour slides from the Queensland Department of Tourism, many books and little trinkets to give away. Although it had nothing whatsoever to do with Geography, I also gave my classmates some sample packs of Vegemite for them to try. It was as foreign a taste to them as marinated herrings were to me. It had been a whirlwind first week at school and one I knew I would never forget.

That Friday was also the date of my first Rotary meeting with the Aarhus Nordvestre Rotary Club. I introduced myself by speaking a few words of Danish, but then had to revert to English when presenting the Club President with the banner of Rotary District 9640. Rotary clubs, and Rotary districts, have banners made from all types of material, from silk and cotton to nylon and other such materials. Rotarians would often exchange their home club's banner when visiting other clubs around the world and then, upon their return home, would present the banner they had received in exchange to their own club. The meetings of the Aarhus Nordvestre Rotary Club were lunchtime meetings, similar to those of my sponsor club in Australia, the Mermaid Beach Rotary Club. Lunch was delightful, even though I was still unfamiliar with much of the menu. In the beverages department, however, I was acutely aware of what was contained in the green bottles with the green and white labels. Again, I was confronted with a delicate decision to make when offered a Grøn Tuborg beer to have with lunch. It became a much less difficult decision to make, however, when it was the Club President offering the beer. Although, after the first couple of mouthfuls, I wondered whether it had been a test. It wasn't. I was grateful for the fact that I felt so comfortable with all the members of my host club despite not being able to understand much of what many of them were saying. I made a point of trying to attend as many of the weekly meetings as I could in an otherwise extremely busy schedule.

It had indeed been a very busy week, having made new friends at school, learning bus routes and timetables and meeting the members of my host Rotary club. Erik's invitation to join him and some of his friends on a night on the town was a welcome opportunity to unwind after such a wonderful week. It was also an opportunity to discover the local bars, nightclubs and snooker halls of Aarhus. While I was not a particularly gifted snooker player, that status changed throughout the year as I became a rather frequent visitor to several snooker halls or bars with snooker tables. I reached a level where I participated in several snooker tournaments with varying degrees of success. Erik and I arrived at the party on time, and it was already in full swing. After a couple of hours at Søren's place, most of us made our way into the heart of the City to a nightclub called Blitz. It was a popular club that was always very busy on Friday and Saturday nights. Not unlike the famous nightclubs of the Gold Coast, Blitz provided a great atmosphere in which to meet and socialise. Meet and socialise I did, and became very friendly with Liela, who was one of the scantily clad barmaids on duty that evening. Erik and his friends were most impressed by the ease at which I obtained discounted and free drinks from Liela for not only myself, but all of us from the party. Erik surprised me greatly when he told me it was 5:00am, as the night still felt young. However, given that I had found myself lost in the City only the week before, I was more than willing to share a taxi home with him.

4

Family One

Many of the other exchange students quickly lost contact with their short-term host families from Odense. While from my often impossible schedule, I could understand how that could happen, I vowed not to let it happen. I had arranged with Ida when I was still in Odense, that I would assist her move to her new unit in Aarhus if I were able. Earlier in the week I had confirmed that arrangement and agreed to meet her at the unit from which she was moving. Ida was to expect me ready, willing and able to assist her in that endeavour at 8:45am Saturday morning. I was ready, more than willing, but only questionably able to carry her furniture and personal effects up and down numerous flights of stairs, because I had only managed to get about two hours sleep the night before. Despite the self-inflicted disability, I managed to see out the next five hours of moving and was surprisingly happy to receive an icy-cold Ceres beer at the end of it all.

Upon my return home, Erik had yet another invitation for me to join him at a party. This time, however, there was a purpose to the party. It was a big university party to celebrate the end of exams and Erik's classmates were only too happy to have me along. This was especially gratifying, given that the university parties were ordinarily open only to the students of the university. In this sense, they were much like the class parties at the Gymnasium. There was nothing particularly unique about the party other than the fact that I was there. It followed the usual pattern of good music, some drinking games and pleasant company.

The special attention I enjoyed from one of the students was, however, memorable. Her name was Sølveig, and she was 28 years of age. Talking to her was as nerve-racking as any conversation I had ever had before, and this only intensified when she invited me to her room at the university. Sølveig was very artistic, and her many paintings, drawings and photographs were displayed proudly on the walls of her unit. I discovered that her ability to creatively express herself was not only limited to art as she quietly expressed her desires to me. I was so very much out-of-my-depth. She was 28, I had only a month before turned 18, and the difference those ten years represented was not limited to numbers. But unlike with Nora in Odense and Emma before her, I figured that if either of us was vulnerable, it was me. I alone controlled that vulnerability, so I let the moment take us to where her desires had intended. Ulrick and I left the party at 2:00am and headed for yet another nightclub called Downtown. That was a real learning experience for me.

I would always attempt to speak Danish, however with only a minimal command of the language at that time and having enjoyed some local beverages, it was difficult. In the early months, I found myself speaking a combination of Danish and English – sometimes in the one sentence! This attracted many young Danish women who were eager to meet an Aussie. Quite apart from the alcohol, the testosterone of an 18-year-old was feeding my ego. It was no surprise therefore, that I happily accepted the advances of Dita. Standing eye to eye, Dita's personality was as cheeky as she was sexy. We danced and kissed until it was time to go home. Given my lack of ready knowledge of the city and the surrounding suburbs, I declined Dita's offer to spend what little was left of the night at her house. That, and the fact that only hours earlier I was swept up in a moment beyond my wildest dreams – a repeat of which I doubted was possible – especially in the same night. The all-night parties, nightclubbing and socialising with friends continued on a regular basis for the entire period of exchange. In fact, there were too many instances on exchange than I care to remember, where a night out ended with the rising of the sun or the start of school the next day. While some of the adventures of these nights and parties warrant description, they were not the fundamental purpose of my time in Denmark and cannot therefore demand telling in their own right. Suffice it to say, in keeping with the proposition that time was more intense on exchange, so too were the social aspects of a late teen.

I certainly enjoyed many nights out with Erik, but he was responsible for showing me so much more than simply the city's nightlife. He truly accepted me as a brother and introduced me as such to all his friends and wider social network. I would often go to the service station nearby and help him close up when he was working on the late shift, or attend university events with him. We also enjoyed other activities such as ice skating. On one such visit to the ice-skating centre, I was approached by a local amateur film crew who were making a parody of the movie *Wuthering Heights*. The person who played the character Cathy was skating towards the person playing the role of Heathcliff, when, just as Cathy arrived at Heathcliff's open arms, ducked under them to embrace the person standing just behind him. That person was me! Being new to the ice, however, meant that it took a few takes for 'Cathy' to be able to embrace me and spin on the spot, without me falling over. In mid-February, Erik was even able to teach me how to build a snowman in the back yard. I woke to see a steady fall of snow and was eager to get outside and enjoy it. I was clumsily trying to make a snowman when Erik showed me how to start by making a small ball of snow and then basically rolling it around in the rest of the snow to gradually increase the diameter of the ball of snow. In doing so, the body of the snowman was created. I also went out to the street and made dozens of small snowballs, before positioning them in such a way to create messages to those at home. One message read, "Hi Dad", another "Hi Mum" and yet another, "Hi All".

Before embarking on exchange and while on it, I understood the purpose of it was to be an ambassador for youth exchange and an ambassador for Australian youth. To fulfil this role, I had been briefed by Rotary, by my family and friends and by other students who had returned from exchange themselves. I had an abundance of information at my disposal, but it didn't always fit. There is arguably no other experience as profound as exchange – especially when sustained over a 12-month period – and it is as uniquely personal as a fingerprint. It is for this reason that fulfilling my purpose as an exchange student could not be guided by any checklist of behaviour or undertakings, but instead revealed itself in a variety of ways as I was confronted with new and challenging experiences. Almost every day of exchange was an adventure in some way, shape or form.

Fundamental and common to most, if not all, exchanges is the very special relationship that students develop with their host families. Attempting to describe the relationship is impossible and a comparison to other relationships is simply futile. In my experience, however, the love and respect that develops within the host family is akin to that within a student's own family far away. If that degree of connection was made within a student's exchange, then it was my opinion that one of the primary purposes of exchange was fulfilled. Luckily for me, the relationships I developed with each of my host families were that special.

Bendt and Clara had a son on exchange in the USA who was about my age. His absence made way for me being hosted by Bendt and Clara, a fact for which I was extremely grateful. Each of my days with Bendt, Clara and Erik saw me grow closer to them and become one of the family. We would regularly take small daytrips as a family and enjoy social occasions together. Given that nothing is too far away in Denmark, some of the day trips enabled wonderful visits to places of interest. Only about 40 kilometres away from home was a neighbouring town called Silkeborg, and it was from there that we caught the world's oldest coal-fired paddle-steamer to Himmelbjerget. The SS Hjejlen was a delightful boat with a rich history. Since her launch 131 years earlier, she had carried Royalty, the local mail and thousands of tourists to Himmelbjerget. Otherwise known as Sky Mountain, this was one of Denmark's highest mountains, although at only 147 metres high, it was not a mountain by the more common understanding of the term. In fact, it was some 2000 metres smaller than Australia's highest mountain.

Three days in early February were especially noteworthy. Bendt, Clara, Erik, his girlfriend, Maja and I went as a family to Copenhagen to help celebrate Clara's father's 80th birthday. It was a long journey, which took around four hours to complete on the road and on a ferry. I had not been feeling too well in the days leading up to the trip, so I took plenty of Vegemite with me. The breakfast spread, popular in Australia, was almost universally detested in Denmark. I was surprised, therefore, when Clara's mother tried some Vegemite with her toasted bread roll and declared, "det smager godt" (it tastes good). After breakfast, we all went on an extensive tour through the capital and saw such things as the Queen's Palace, Parliament House, the harbour, the State Library and the National Cathedral. Everything was just so impressive, especially when nearly all the sights pre-dated the colonisation of my own country. The National Cathedral, known by the Danes as Vor Frue Kirke or the Church of Our Lady, was spectacular. It was around 83 metres long, over 30 metres wide and from the floor to the ceiling inside, some 25 metres high. Standing on marble bases down each side of the main hall were statues of the twelve Apostles and between them, rows upon rows of solid timber pews. There were elaborate gold candelabra mounted on timber posts at each end of the pews, and the decorative carvings throughout were extraordinary. I was particularly taken by the experience of watching the changing of the guard at the Queen's Palace. All the replacement guards would march around the huge, paved area in the front of the Palace, stopping at each guard station to change with their colleagues. I was in awe at both the tradition and precision involved in this regular exercise of duty for the Royal Guards. Despite being rather tired from the long day sight-seeing, we all enjoyed the birthday party that evening. It was not a raucous affair, which is not surprising given it was an 80th birthday party but was enjoyable.

Many exchange students visited me in Aarhus. It was not surprising that I had so many visitors, because Aarhus was often known as the party city. Having such a large student population, bolstered by the nation's second-largest university, ensured that there was a vibrant youth scene in Aarhus. But of all the students who visited, Matthew was the first. Matthew and I had quickly developed a strong friendship in Odense and had maintained regular contact over those early weeks following language course. His first visit, which over the course of the year became the first of very many visits, was perhaps the most memorable.

After meeting at the train station, Matthew and I went directly to Hanne's house to watch a video and to introduce my best friend in Denmark to Matthew. After the video, Hanne told us that she was going out on the town with friends that night and invited us to join her. That night we all sang, danced and drank merrily until the early hours of the morning. While neither of us could sing well, Matthew and I sang several songs at Sam's Bar, which was a dedicated karaoke bar. We introduced ourselves to the packed club and explained that we were exchange students in Denmark for a year. After that, we proceeded to sing *That's What Friends are For* which, given the introduction, was very popularly received. As soon as the next day I couldn't remember the other songs we had sung, because none had been received as emotionally by the crowd. Having been caught out in the city before, I was keen to ensure Matthew and I caught the last night bus home. We boarded the bus and joined only the driver and one other passenger. At the next stop, however, two girls boarded the bus. We started talking with them and, to my surprise, discovered that they both lived in my street. Laerke and Majken had been friends for many years, attended the same school and for most of their lives lived in the same street. They actually looked rather similar with their red hair, fair but freckled skin and cute smiles. Both were attractive, but I did find myself attracted in the physical sense to Laerke. She possessed razor-sharp wit, which also ensured talking with her was as enjoyable as spending intimate time with her. By the time we arrived at the bus stop nearest my home, I had already stolen a kiss from Laerke. It was an easy invitation to accept, therefore, when Laerke invited Majken, Matthew and myself back to her place for a few more drinks. Laerke lived with her parents, but in an almost separate dwelling from the main house. It was a wonderful night and for Laerke and I, the beginning of a great friendship.

I was reassured that Bendt and Clara had an open and modern view on certain adolescent matters. I had recently met a fellow Australian exchange student who was hosted three hours by train and bus from Aarhus. We had met at an exchange student gathering and discovered an immediate attraction. Leanne was as close to an angel as we of the living will ever get. Her long straight blonde hair was as enticing as her captivating eyes, and her lips were as soft as silk. We had both been very mindful of the guidelines by which we lived our lives and shared only a sleeping bag at the gathering those weeks before. However, we were in private when Leanne came to stay with me at Bendt and Clara's home. I met Leanne at the train station Friday afternoon and went straight home to introduce her to my wonderful host family. I was so proud of my relationship with them and eagerly introduced other exchange students to them. I knew from our time together previously that the weekend was going to test the resolve we had shown when sharing her sleeping bag. We enjoyed a lovely dinner with my host family before embarking on a night of fun and mirth in the city.

Leanne was impressed by the number of local contacts I had made in the relatively short time I had been in Aarhus. The way I was able to introduce her to nightclub managers, bar and wait staff in several different venues and generally be known to many, indicated to Leanne, and to myself, that I was well on the way to becoming Danish. Back at home, my room was immediately next to Leanne's but even that seemed too far away. Leanne asked me to share her room, her bed and her body and we unleashed the passion that had built up within us over not only that night but also in the weeks following our previous meeting. At that stage of my life, I had only enjoyed a few partners against whom I could relate the experience with Leanne. All I knew was that Leanne was entirely uninhibited and very adventurous. It was a night that I knew would be re-lived several times over in my mind. Our feelings were clearly visible to my host family, yet despite this, no objections were raised.

Easter arrived with astonishing speed. I remember thinking, *how could it be Easter, I haven't been here that long.* I was informed a couple of weeks earlier over dinner with Bendt, Clara and Erik that we were going to spend Easter in the Alsace region of northern France. I had not been to France before and the prospect of doing so was exciting. On Saturday, 11th of April 1992 we departed for France. We were also joined by Erik's girlfriend, Maja. She was a very kind and sincere person and quickly accepted me as a close friend.

One of the many attractions of Europe became evident during our drive to France – so much diversity in such relatively small distances. Although the destination for our Easter vacation was France, we visited German cities and towns such as Hamburg, Hanover, Dortmund, Cologne and Bonn along the way. It was truly amazing that within 50 kilometres either side of a country's border, such dramatic differences could be identified. Sure, the landscapes either side of the national borders did not change in any significant way, but the language, currency, food and people most certainly did. My host family were also good enough to take me to Frankfurt. It was an impressive city, which was not surprising given it was not only the financial centre of Germany but also the largest financial centre in continental Europe. The autobahn interchange at Frankfurt was one of the most heavily used in all of Europe and that was certainly true of our visit. There were hundreds of cars making full use of the high-speed highways leading in and out of Frankfurt. Of all the German cities and towns that we visited on our travels south, the one that I was most excited to see was Düsseldorf. It was famous for its cultural and trade fairs, but for me, it was the fact that it was a city referred to regularly in one of my favourite television shows growing up. *Hogan's Heroes* was a television programme that finished filming before I was even born but was one that grabbed my attention as a child. While there was nothing at all familiar about Düsseldorf when I visited, it was still a highlight for me having simply been there.

While an entire holiday could be based in and around those cities and towns, France and, in particular, the small region of Alsace was our ultimate destination. It didn't take very long at all for us to arrive after crossing the border into France. As we weaved our way up and along the sloping hillside on which the holiday house was built, the view grew more and more spectacular. As we neared the house, we could look down into the valley below and see lush, green land lined with vineyards and buildings from a time long past. Finally, we reached the holiday house, and it too was historic. Engraved in the sandstone facade was the date 1851. The polished timber beams and finishings inside the house had not let age weary them and the furnishings were true to the style of previous generations. I was entirely spoiled in that I had a large queen-sized, four-poster bed and a quilt filled with the finest down.

The next day we were all up bright and early as we had a great deal of sight-seeing to do. We drove to Strasbourg, home to such sights as the monument to Gutenberg and Cathedral de Nôtre-Dame. Gutenberg, who was widely credited with the invention of the printing press, was celebrated in Strasbourg by a stately bronze statue made in 1840. He was depicted holding a page printed with the Old Testament verse *Et la lumiere fut* (and there was light). Four large bronze inserts complemented the statue at its base, all of which illustrated the benefits resulting from the invention of the printing press. Cathedral de Nôtre-Dame was, for me, one of the most incredible Gothic buildings in Europe. Rising some 142 metres to its pinnacle, the Cathedral boasted an impressive and intricate iconographic facade, together with the world's largest circular lead-light. The great rose window was almost 14 metres in diameter. It was truly remarkable, particularly since construction commenced in 1277 before the advent of technology and other modern building practices. It has often been joked that a European holiday consists mainly of visiting old churches, but I must say from my experience, nothing was further from the truth. I must also say that visiting churches was wonderfully inspiring. Cathedral de Nôtre-Dame was not only a religious house, but it was an architectural masterpiece, the history of which was older than the very nation in which I was born. Modern architects, engineers and builders rarely build structures with as much intricate detail as some of these historic buildings, yet they have the advantage of modern technology with which to do so. The satisfaction from visiting not only churches, but any building of that era was simply awesome.

Strasbourg, though, had far more to offer than culturally spectacular sights and the seemingly endless canals. Its significant importance to European politics caught my attention and demanded further exploration. Luckily, my host family was also particularly interested in such things, especially given Erik was studying political science at university. Almost immediately upon the end of World War II, the major western European nations decided it was prudent to establish a united European organisation and collectively chose Strasbourg as its headquarters. Several European Council buildings were built over the following 10 to 20 years, including the Palais des Droits de l'Homme, the Palace of Human Rights. It wasn't until 1967, however, that construction of the Palais de l'Europe was complete. It housed not only the very large Hall of Parliament but also the many offices and common areas needed for the proper operation of the European Council. As a result, the entire complex was very substantial and an impressive place to visit. Interestingly, I learnt that despite construction being completed in 1967, it took more than a decade for the representatives elected by the people of the member nations, to actually meet in the great Hall of Parliament.

Time is a valuable commodity when on holiday, so we wasted little of it over a short lunch in a quaint little French cafe before leaving Strasbourg. Upon leaving Strasbourg, we ventured to an extraordinary castle that has witnessed so much of history, that many volumes of historical text could be written about the castle alone. The first records of Chateau Haut-Koenigsbourg dated back to around 1147, but the castle unsuccessfully endured the Thirty Years War and suffered some two hundred years in ruins. Throughout its full history, the castle occupied both French and Germany territory as country borders were driven back and forth during times of war and conflict. It wasn't until after a complete reconstruction in 1908 that the government awarded the castle its status as a National Palace in 1919. While during times of war or strife, the strategic position of the castle on a ridge of the Vosges Mountains lent itself to good defence, it provided us with a spectacular view over the Alsace Plain 757 metres below. Chateau Haut-Koenigsbourg not only took my breath away, but it also took all our remaining time that day. On our drive home, we visited one of the many vineyards in the region and sampled the exquisite wines on offer. We purchased two bottles of red and two of white and returned to our hillside holiday house.

Our travels the following day were seriously hampered by the poor weather conditions and all we could achieve was a visit to where the Moselle River starts its impressive and long journey from little more than a trickle. It flows through France and Luxembourg before meeting the Rhine River in Germany. The site was marked at a small monument just off to the side of Route des Sources, which was the road leading from the village of Bussang up to and beyond the monument. The village and the monument, only minutes away, were located high on the western slope of the Ballon d'Alsace, which was one of the large mountains on the border of the Alsace and Lorraine regions of France. While I couldn't read French, I was able to decipher from the bronze plaque mounted on the sandstone wall that the monument was called 'Source de la Moselle' and was positioned at an altitude of 715 metres. At its source, the Moselle River bubbled through a sandstone 'L' shaped wall set into the earth behind and above the monument. From a little pond at the foot of the wall, the water then trickled into a small man-made 'gutter', no deeper than perhaps two or three centimetres and bordered by hundreds of rectangular stones of no more than about half a metre in length and 10 or 15 centimetres wide. I was told that many bicycle tours visited the location during the summer months. The most famous bicycle race in the world passed through the region in the first official mountain climb of the Tour de France in July 1905. I had ridden up some hills and mountains in my time, especially during my ride from Sydney to the Gold Coast, but I was amazed that cyclists were able to conquer those mountains. I felt privileged to be able to stand at the source of such a famous river and, while I didn't know it at the time, I would get to see it at the other end of its flow later in the holiday.

All is rarely lost as a result of poor weather. After returning from Bussang, we simply enjoyed each other's company with games of table-tennis and cards well into the evening. We savoured wine and cheese sourced locally and had a lovely dinner of traditional French cuisine. We also spent a good deal of time simply talking to each other. I had long felt that I could safely express my feelings, goals and views with my beautiful host family and this feeling was only strengthened during those hours spent indoors. It was certainly an opportunity to immerse myself in 'hygge'. Hygge is a Danish word that has no direct English translation but is very much a defining characteristic of Danish culture. Broadly speaking, it might be described as cosiness or a sense of contentment. Over the course of the year, I formed the view that it is about being present and connected – to enable that feeling of contentment to flourish. In many ways, that day was as much a highlight of the holiday as any other and was yet a further indication in my mind that I was 'becoming Danish'. I went to bed that night, content in the knowledge that I was a part of the family and that the family would always be a part of me.

When we first arrived at our French retreat, I had discovered an old toboggan hanging on the wall of the garage. It wasn't as old as the house but had clearly carried many a person down mountain slopes. Although it was Easter and certainly cold enough, there was no snow when we arrived. On our fifth day, however, I woke to see the pine-tree forest below covered with fluffy white snow. The sturdy green treetops battled bravely to break through the thick white coverings laid upon them by the inclement weather but largely without success. The ground, too, was blanketed by the sky's own powder and was not blemished by markings of any kind. My thoughts turned immediately to the toboggan I had seen and went outside to make full use of it. Erik and Maja were content to let me discover the best areas on the slope for tobogganing before joining in for a little over an hour of fun. I had not used a toboggan on snow before, only on the massive sand hills of the world's largest sand island, Fraser Island. The first few rides down the hill identified for me the fastest and most exciting paths and enabled me to get a good feel for how best to manoeuvre the toboggan. My repeated use of virtually the same areas of the slope, also compacted the snow and made the tracks icier and faster.

We couldn't spend too much time on the toboggan as we were again going to attempt the drive up to the summit of the Vosges Mountains. While the Route des Crêtes, or road of the peaks was still slippery, it and the other roads weren't completely blocked by snow as they were the previous days. We trekked to the summit of the Grand Ballon from where the view of the Alsatian Plain and the Black Forest was simply extraordinary. On clear days in summer, it was possible to see over to Austria, Liechtenstein and Mont Blanc. In winter, the Grand Ballon was generally the coldest and windiest point in all of Alsace. From our visit, I could well believe that fact. Not only was there thick snow covering the ground, but the monument erected in memory of all the soldiers that fought in the mountains during the First World War had thick wind-blown icicles sticking out sideways from the side. The monument had weathered years of severe conditions, but it also had a history of its own. It was first constructed in 1927 but was then stolen by the Nazis in 1940 before being rebuilt in 1960. The descent from the summit was considerably faster for me than it was for my host family. I was face down on a plastic bag, sliding at great speed over the snowy slope of the mountain. At eighteen years of age and with an unbridled sense of adventure, I thought it would be fun. As I hurtled toward the roadside car park, I realised that I had built up a great deal of momentum and had no way of stopping. So, I simply dug my unprotected hands into the snow, which acted as a catapult and sent me into a disorientating spin head over heels. I did manage to stop, but my hands were blue from the cold, and it was feared I was suffering from frostbite. Holding a warm cup of soup in the mountainside cafeteria soon brought feeling back to my hands and pleased my palate at the same time.

    Our holiday in France quickly drew to a close, and we found ourselves back on the road heading for Denmark. The only overnight stop on our return trip was in the town of Cochem, positioned alongside the Moselle River. We stayed at the Konditorei Hotel, which was certainly impressive with its grey slate tiles cladding the outside walls of the ground floor and apricot coloured cement render for the four levels above. The interior, with an accent on timber, was equally appealing. As impressive as it was, it was not nearly as impressive as the imperial castle perched high above the town. Reichsburg Cochem was one of those must-see attractions along the Moselle. Earliest records suggest that it was constructed around the year 1000, although it was torched and reduced to a ruin in 1689. It remained that way until it was rebuilt in 1868. The view of Cochem from the castle, some 100 metres above, was spectacular as were the vast interior features. There were period weapons and a large boar's head mounted above an enormous fireplace, which itself was the feature of the elaborate and expansive great hall. We were all in awe at the castle. I had enjoyed both Modern and Ancient History subjects at school, but I never really *felt* that history. I simply stood still at various locations throughout the castle and just imagined the history around me coming alive. Aided by that vivid imagination, I felt the rich and long history of the castle. There were dinner tours available at the castle, but we had already made reservations for dinner in the splendid Konditorei Hotel's signature restaurant. After a most delicious and traditionally German dinner, Erik, Maja and I made our way out to savour some local nightlife. I had already come to the realisation that, in Denmark, the nightclubs there were not vastly different from those at home, and this was equally true for the nightclub we visited in Cochem. What was unique though, was how the nightclub sought to remain efficient with service at the bar. Upon entry, patrons were able to purchase drink cards, which would simply be 'clipped' when ordering each drink at the bar. That way, the bar staff didn't have to handle any money. We only stayed for two or three drinks before retiring to our room back at the hotel.

Bendt and Clara had certainly left no stone unturned in planning an itinerary of the highest interest as we visited various German sights on the final day of our homeward journey. Of particular interest was the town of Koblenz and the large memorial constructed at the confluence of the magnificent Moselle River and the romantic Rhine River. The monument was erected with the desire for a unified Germany and only a short distance behind the monument were three pieces of the Berlin Wall. Each of the three separate pieces of the wall had bronze plates affixed to them with the inscriptions: *17 Juni 1953*; *Den Opfern der Teilung* and *9 November 1989* in that order. The first date in 1953 represented the date of the first attempt at reunification of Western and Eastern Germany, which was violently suppressed and in which many people died. Translated, the inscription on the middle piece of the wall said, *Dedicated to the victims of separation* and the date in 1989 on the third piece of the wall was when the Berlin Wall finally and famously came down, and East Germany opened its borders once more to the West. The many bullet holes in those pieces of the wall were a stark reminder to me of the horrors of that period in German history. Again, to *feel* the history represented by those pieces of the wall was to do more than simply look at, touch and photograph them.

During our nine-day Easter adventure, I had seen and stood where the Moselle River started, where it met the great Rhine River in Koblenz and had experienced so many other wonderful sights in between. Most importantly though, the time spent with my beloved host family allowed me to grow even closer to them. I certainly tried to reduce my appreciation to words, but they were really insufficient. I truly loved our Easter holiday in the same way I truly loved my host family.

Upon our return from France, I set aside an entire day to simply sit down and write letters about our Easter holiday. On that occasion, I wrote thirteen different letters and two postcards. It occurred to me that such prodigious letter writing would occupy too much of my time if I did that regularly. I decided, from that point forward, I would either write or type my letters and then photocopy them as many times as needed. To those photocopies I would add personal messages to the individual recipient, but the bulk of the letter would be common across all recipients. This made abundant sense to me, especially since there was so much repetition across the individually prepared letters.

At my first opportunity, I also spoke in thanks of Bendt and Clara at my Rotary club. Although I had done so privately, I wanted to thank them publicly for what had been an amazing Easter experience. Indeed, giving thanks before my Rotary club for things large or small that my host families or other members of the club did for me, was something I found myself doing regularly. An interesting and somewhat serendipitous pattern began to emerge from such gestures – the more I gave thanks, the more I was given. So profound was this discovery, that I resolved then and there, that this was a formula that could and should be applied to life beyond exchange.

I cherished every day that I was a member of Bendt and Clara's family. It was because of that love of the family, that leaving them for an eighteen-day tour of Europe was so difficult. I was inextricably torn between the excitement that the Euro-Tour was to provide, but sadly aware that upon my return, I would have only seven days left with Bendt and Clara. That return came all too soon, and I was faced with my final week of living with my first family.

During that precious and final week, I spent three days in the nation's capital with Erik and his friend, Christian. One of their close friends, Thomas, had moved to Copenhagen for work about six months earlier and was celebrating his birthday. We had to leave Aarhus very early, because the combination of transportation by bus, ferry and train ensured the trip from Aarhus to Copenhagen was a long one – several hours. Thomas lived in a suburb called Charlottelund, about ten minutes' drive outside the heart of the city and very close to the world's oldest amusement park, called Dyrehavsbakken. Bakken, as it was more commonly known, was our ultimate destination after having met Thomas at his house and dropping off our luggage.

The amusement park seemed to almost have a personality of its own, developed over hundreds of years by many individual tent owners throughout the park. I talked to an Australian man who had, some 15 years earlier, met and married a Danish lady and her family was one of the tent owners. There were over fifty self-employed business owners who each ran their own part of the park, and the traditional reference to them as tent owners remained the business designation to that day. Bakken first opened in 1583 and quickly became a cultural attraction with a popular circus revue and music hall drawing visitors from all over Denmark and beyond. As its popularity grew, investment was made by new tent owners in the more modern and exciting amusements that were there on my visit. Of those amusements, the rollercoaster was perhaps the crowning glory. Just as Bakken was the oldest amusement park in the world, the roller-coaster, too, was one of the oldest. It was built in 1932 and was made almost entirely from timber – the rails, the cross-members, the posts, the carriages – all timber. Because it was timber, there were no loops but certainly enough twists, turns and plummeting drops to rapidly active the adrenalin. The creaking and cracking sounds made by those old timbers as the carriages raced over them simply added to the very excitement of the ride. Given that we had all enjoyed a rather large meal and several beers before attending the park, we were careful not to repeat the rides too many times. That approach also ensured that we experienced virtually all the attractions of the park, before it closed at midnight.

Despite a late night, we were all up quite early the next day. I'd like to say that it was the discipline of wanting to explore Copenhagen, but it was because we were woken not once, but twice, by others. The first was the cleaner for the house in which Thomas rented the basement, while the second was another friend of theirs who had arrived from England earlier than planned. So, we took full advantage of the early morning and went into the city to explore it further. I remembered many of the sights from my earlier visit with Clara and Bendt, such as the Queen's Palace. This time I saw some new landmarks, most notable of which was The Little Mermaid. A petite statue, measuring only 1.25 metres in height, sat on a large granite plinth, which in turn was positioned atop a few large rocks just beyond the water line of the Copenhagen Harbour. The statue was inspired, of course, by the famous Hans Christian Andersen fairy tale of the same name. Actually, it was inspired by the ballet adaptation of the fairy tale. It was commissioned by Carl Jacobsen, the son of the founder of the famous Carlsberg brewery. He had attended the theatre ballet performance of

The Little Mermaid and was so taken by the prima ballerina Ellen Price, that she was asked to model for the statue. She agreed, but for the head only. The sculptor Edvard Eriksen asked his wife to model nude for the body. She obliged and in August 1913, the unimposing bronze statue was unveiled to the Danish public. I was in awe of the small, yet iconic figure. She had withstood the perils of time, weather and even vandalism for almost 80 years and was as much an attraction to local and foreign tourists then, as she was when unveiled all those years prior.

After a few more hours of sightseeing, we returned to Thomas' house. There I was introduced to yet another drinking game. While normally such games wouldn't find a place in my diary, other than by reference to them having been played, this one did. It was simple by design, but difficult in practice. Open beers would be placed ten metres apart and competitors would consume the first open beer. They would then place the empty bottle on the ground, bend down with a finger in or on the top of the empty bottle and run around it three times. They would then run the ten metres and consume the next beer and repeat the same action, before running back to the original point to drink yet another beer and so it would continue. Once a player fell over or became sick, they would be out of the game. The player remaining standing, or first to finish his allocation of beer, would be the winner. An ounce irresponsible perhaps, but it was ultimately some harmless bonding with good friends and quite simply, good fun. That night stretched into the early hours of the next day and with that, our return to Aarhus.

Having spent those adventure-filled days with Erik in Copenhagen, I was left facing the final days with Bendt and Clara. My last full day was Sunday, 31 May 1992 and it was spent in the most relaxing fashion imaginable. Erik and I rode into town, met Christian and Tina and joined them for a drive to the beach. It was my first visit to a Danish beach – at least for the purposes of swimming and play – and was very much an eye-opener. It was so very different to going to the beach at home, not only because of the lack of waves and the very cold water, but because nearly all the women were without tops. Not only were they enjoying sunbathing topless but were swimming and playing beach sports in the same fashion. We spent several hours simply basking in the sun and enjoying what was perhaps one of the finest days of weather I had experienced in Denmark. Of course, the sun has to set – not only on a day, but metaphorically on a period of my Danish life. That night, I found myself sharing a farewell dinner with the family at a delightfully quaint inn, only minutes from our home. Built in 1825, Aarslev Krogaard was originally one of Denmark's largest and most extraordinary inns and was still, at the time of my visit, a very popular destination for travellers and business executives. We ate exceptionally fine food and enjoyed quality wine, before returning home to further enjoy each other's company.

We sat on the porch just out from the living room, accompanied by Vanja, our faithful dog. We spent hours just talking and laughing before the mood changed with more sombre overtones. Bendt stood to address us all, but more specifically his comments were directed toward me. He spoke with impassioned enthusiasm about how the family enjoyed the time I had spent with them and how they loved me as one of their own. Fighting the tears was one of the hardest fights I had ever fought and was one I was proud to have lost. The 'knock-out punch' came when Bendt and Clara presented me with Thor's Hammer. A solid ingot of sterling silver, the necklace pendant represented the mythical hammer used by Thor, the God in Norse Mythology of lightning and thunder. The giving of the necklace was accompanied by the words, "you are and always will be, a son of this house." The emotion of those few minutes was overwhelming. It was brought about by a unique combination of abundant happiness, sadness and love. There was no doubt in my mind that my love for my host family was equalled by theirs for me and that they too would be sad to see me move on to my next host family. I remembered the words of a wise Rotarian during one of my briefing camps, who said, "on exchange, don't be sad that it's over, but be happy that it occurred in the first place." My time with Bendt and Clara had elevated me to a higher awareness of myself and of others and awakened in me a greater understanding of cultural diversity. It demonstrated time and again that I had a natural capacity for learning and adapting. It confirmed unequivocally that life as a teenage exchange student is lived more intensely than it normally would without exchange. Importantly, it assured me that it was safe to experience life in that heightened way and surrender to the immersion. That was the abundant happiness that I decided to take with me.

The next day was spent packing my bags for yet another move in what was quickly becoming a disappearing year. In moments of private solitude as I packed, I reflected tearfully on those first marvellous months of my exchange that had passed so rapidly. It was so difficult to reconcile how, only months before, I perceived twelve months of exchange as a long time – a great challenge – but at that point, realised it was not long enough. By mid-afternoon, my room looked like it did the day I arrived, my bags were packed, and I was ready to move to Højberg and join Carl and Marie's family. Bendt and Clara drove me across town to my new Højberg address, where Carl and Marie welcomed me with open arms and warm hearts.

5

Euro Extravaganza

The adventure that so unwittingly stole eighteen days from the last few weeks with Bendt and Clara's family was the 'Euro-Tour'. Rotary left nothing to chance in ensuring every exchange student had the opportunity to experience untold excitement and discover parts of the world they might never have seen otherwise. To achieve that, Rotary organised a bus tour of Europe. Three buses left various parts of Denmark at staggered starts, a few days between each. The trip was not only a tour of European countries but a voyage of discovery and learning. On each bus, two Rotary chaperones were on hand to escort, supervise and counsel students.

Bendt and Clara drove me to the rendezvous point which was in the car park of the Aarhus concert hall. A number of other students had gathered there, as Aarhus was one of the major pick-up stops for the bus. Shortly after we arrived, the giant yellow Tjæreborg bus eased to a halt before us. It was about half full with other exchange students from throughout the mainland north of Aarhus. Tjæreborg was a specialist tour operator in Denmark, renowned for custom-designed tour packages throughout Europe. They had continuously improved the tour over several years and had created an extremely thorough itinerary. I boarded the bus and found seats with Matthew and Michael, who were also catching the bus from Aarhus. My backpack was full to the zippers with food, beer, camera, walkman, dictaphone and other little necessary trinkets. Our Rotary chaperones were not joining our group until a pick-up point further to the south. At the final stop, more students boarded what was now a very full bus. The official count of exchange students was 54, made up predominantly by Australians; but also included students from New Zealand, Canada, the USA and Japan. The gender balance on tour was also distinctly in favour of the females. Of the students on the tour, only 15 of them were male. Of course, I had no problem with that at all and didn't hear any of the other males take issue with it either.

I didn't notice our Rotary chaperones board the bus and was caught quite by surprise when I discovered that I had just offered one of them a beer. As it turned out, our Rotary chaperones had been on youth exchange not too many years prior. They were as eager to enjoy the tour as we were. Although the rule was meant to be that no alcohol was to be taken on the bus, much less consumed on it, Carsten and Pernille were happy to allow it in moderation. Early in the trip and for reasons I never discovered, Carsten and Pernille were nicknamed 'King Bart' and 'Queen Pee Pee' and that was how they were generally addressed for the remainder of the tour. It occurred to me that Carsten's nickname may have stemmed from the fact he looked very much like 'Bart Simpson' from the animated television series, *The Simpsons*, but I never asked. The root of Pernille's nickname was, to me, a mystery and, in any event, both nicknames were in jest.

Our first stop was at the border between Denmark and Germany. Many of the exchange students who had not had the good fortune of travelling with their host families were eager to have the German border control stamp added to their passports. Luckily for me, I had already obtained it when travelling to France with Bendt and Clara. Because we had been told we could enjoy alcohol in moderation while on tour, at the first stop, which was alongside a roadside liquor market, Matthew, Paulina, Annalise, Richard and I all pooled our money and bought an enormous magnum of Cinzano and a case of beer for consumption during our first evening on tour. The prices were considerably cheaper than in Denmark and the little money we had spare seemed to go a long way.

We knew we were not staying in Sheraton hotels on tour, but the backpackers' accommodations were mostly comfortable. This was not the case on our first night in the former East Berlin. In fact, it was plainly obvious that the re-unification of East and West Germany, only a few years prior, had not had any visible, positive effects in terms of the standard of available accommodation. Our room of four beds had giant windows that opened completely out, so much so that one could sit on the windowsill. The view from that window was of a scarcely-used section of railway track, littered everywhere with discarded bed mattresses, overflowing rubbish bins, rusted car bodies and broken glass. The view inside was not much better with paint peeling from the concrete walls that were showing signs of concrete rot, linoleum floors and old steel-framed beds with tired springs that squeaked with the slightest movement. The amenities were not exempt from the general state of disrepair and they were probably the worst. One had to be careful not to move too much when sitting on the toilet as it had broken completely free of its fixture to the floor. The shower recess was dirty, but after removing the dead rat, it was passable. The living conditions though, impacted little on the evening as the company of good friends, many of them recently made, was the focal point. I had long before met Matthew, but together we became friends with Paulina, Annalise and Richard, with whom we shared the beer purchased at the border. These three were from the USA and had been on exchange for nine months. We did not drink the Cinzano as Paulina knocked it over and smashed it on the floor in our room. Shards of thick emerald-green glass made the prospect of recovering the beverage impossible, not to mention the filthy floor from which it was mopped. We were grateful though for small blessings as the smell of the Cinzano that had flooded our floor was more appealing than the otherwise offensive odour of the room.

At breakfast the next morning, it was apparent that the cooking was only slightly better than the accommodation and I chose to skip it. I was not alone in that decision and luckily so, as several students fell ill over the course of the day. We couldn't say for sure whether it was the food, but had I been a betting man, I would have wagered it was. We then departed our hostel and headed into the city. The many statues and monuments in and around the city of Berlin, both the Eastern and Western parts, proved to be quite the attraction for most of the students on tour. A select few of us found the monuments to be more akin to playground equipment as we climbed in and on them, searching always for that unique photo opportunity. The grand concert house that stands proudly in the Gendarmenmarket was not only spectacular but was also one such photo opportunity. Either side of the enormous front stairs were two large statues atop large sandstone pillars. The one on the right, looking at the building, was a stately bronzed lion, with a winged angel riding side-saddle on its back. The intricate detail of the statue was impressive, as too was my effort in climbing undiscovered up and onto the neck of the lion. At that point I was about six or seven metres, perhaps higher still, from the ground of the Gendarmenmarket. The Konzerthaus (Concert House) was one of the most recent of the buildings in the market square or Gendarmenmarket. Despite that description, it still had a history dating back to construction in 1821. Of course, during the Second World War, it suffered severe damage as did neighbouring buildings around the Gendarmenmarket and was finally reconstructed in 1984. I was always acutely aware of the risks around safety and perhaps even the legality of such activity but wanted my photos to say more than simply, *I was there,* or *I saw that.* Because it has been said that 'a picture paints a thousand words', I wanted there to be a story to as many of my photographs as possible, something to make them uniquely mine. If that meant putting myself in the photos in some slightly questionable ways, then I was prepared to do so. Nobody seemed to mind and had there been any objection raised, I would have respected the objection.

After a general orientation tour of the city, which exposed us to the major sights such as the Brandenburg Gate, Checkpoint Charlie, parts of the remaining Berlin Wall and the Reichstag, we were permitted to choose from two or three different options for the afternoon. Berlin really was a place where you could take a turn at any corner and discover a history lesson. A discerning handful of us chose to visit the Berlin Zoo instead, which was a decision devoid of any regret. We were certainly more excited to be there than the animals were but only arguably better behaved. The Berlin Zoo was, at the time, one of the largest zoos in the world with over 1400 different species of animal. The animal statues located throughout the zoo fell victim to the same quest for those unique photo opportunities that had befallen some of the buildings within the city. Without question though, was the unique photo opportunity that presented itself as Matthew, Richard, Paulina and I arrived at the lion enclosure. Whether it was destiny, coincidence or sheer good fortune, we arrived only moments before they were about to put an adorable lion cub away in the enclosure with its mother. After some pleading from the four of us, the attendant allowed us to not only have our photographs taken holding the cub but to spend several minutes simply playing with it in the sandy enclosure away from its mother.

I had always held mixed views on zoos and other such animal parks. On one hand were the arguments about animal cruelty and the removal of mostly wild animals from their natural environments. On the other hand, were the arguments about animal conservation and educating people about the plight of the cousins of many of the species featured at the zoo. In my mind, where zoos or other keepers of wildlife did so humanely and with proper motivation, then the balance of animal rights and the education of people through attractions such as zoos could indeed be reconciled. I certainly developed a much greater knowledge of, and affinity with, lions than I'd had before that experience. At the end of the day, the lion cub encounter was unquestionably the highlight of my visit to the zoo and perhaps even of my visit to Berlin.

We suspected our hostel had never been as lively as it was when we returned from our day in the city. That characteristic, though, only applied because we had returned with such vigour having enjoyed a great day out. Our enthusiastic demeanour changed somewhat when confronted with yet another meal of questionable quality at the hostel. I had, earlier that day, already passed on breakfast, given its dubious odour and appearance. However, after a day of activities, the kind of which we had experienced, nobody was without a healthy appetite. With no other options available to us, we all braved the evening's meal. It served its purpose but did so without any glowing compliments to the chef. Some things remain rather consistent wherever you go, so we were confident our recently acquired supplies of tequila would be as good as any. Paulina and Annalise joined Matthew, Richard and me in our room, as we 'licked, sipped, sucked' our way to the early hours of the following morning. While I was prepared to 'bend the rules' in relation to the consumption of alcohol, I wasn't willing to do so with the smoking of illicit drugs. My new-found American friends started to smoke, at which time I protested most vociferously. I told the girls, bluntly, that they should go back to their room if they wanted to do that and they could take Richard with them. There was no need to confirm whether I was serious or not, and the drugs were put away. I had no further encounter with drugs that night or at any other time on exchange. My Dad had always said to me, "be a leader not a follower" and despite that being much easier said than done in many circumstances, it was most certainly the right thing to do in that instance. Considering the time we finally got to sleep that night, making the 9:00am departure time the next morning was quite an achievement.

Some 400 kilometres separated Berlin from our next destination, which was Prague in what was then Czechoslovakia. Not only would the drive take up most of the day, but we had two very different sights to see along the way. In little more than a cursory visit, we managed to enjoy the opulence of the Zwinger Palace in Dresden. It was reported to be one of the finest examples of late baroque architecture in the world and a true masterpiece in its class. Completed in 1728, the Palace boasted a plethora of sculptures and statues and amazing gardens making up the central square. The signs and our brochures suggested there were vast artistic holdings, galleries and exhibitions throughout, but our time simply didn't permit such an exploration. In the short time we had though, it did feel very much like a movie set, designed to take the audience back some 200 years.

Few things move a person more than tragedy and suffering. While we didn't suffer directly, visiting a former concentration camp certainly moved us. Many cried. The thousands of concrete headstones in the grounds of the camp were clear reminders of the tragedy that had occurred there. That place was Theresienstadt and was located between Dresden in Germany and Prague in Czechoslovakia. The entrance to the former concentration camp bore the words *Arbeit Macht Frei* (work brings freedom). History, and the guide at Theresienstadt, told us that, of course, the motto was erroneous. Our guides and the various information boards around the camp further confirmed that Theresienstadt was not a 'death camp' but was a work camp. Despite that, almost 100,000 prisoners died 'working' at Theresienstadt. Even though there were none of the abhorrent gas chambers as found at the more notorious camps like Auschwitz, Sobibor or Treblinka, there was still chilling evidence of the crematorium ovens used to dispose of the bodies of those who had died. Up to 190 bodies would be disposed of by cremation daily. I actually found myself struggling with various emotions, from sorrow and disgust to relief and appreciation. The sorrow and disgust were difficult to grapple with as there was no excuse, justification or reasoning that could explain why human beings were treated in such a way. Fortunately, my experience at Theresienstadt was one of retrospection and that permitted me to feel relief that the war and the suffering of those prisoners did finally end. I did, however, appreciate the fact that I had been able to see for myself a part of that terrible period in modern history and take valuable lessons about the fundamental importance of humanity. Theresienstadt was one of those rare places where I was uncomfortable and saddened by what I knew had occurred there decades prior, but I was nonetheless drawn to it for its rich lessons and historical understanding. Several of us were nursing hangovers of varying degrees from the night before and Theresienstadt certainly had a most sobering effect. We felt rather poorly, but there was simply no correlation between our poorly state and the torturous suffering that was endured by tens of thousands of people when the camp was operational. To have drawn any analogy would have been to insult the memory of those that had fallen. I think the distinctly quiet bus ride for several kilometres after we left Theresienstadt was no coincidence.

Czechoslovakia was simply inspirational and its cultural value beyond measure. At the border, customs officers thoroughly searched the bus and conducted random checks of our luggage. The officers were all carrying automatic rifles and were very matter of fact in their behaviour. Even though I knew I had nothing to worry about, the experience of armed officers conducting a search in that manner was still a little disquieting. Shortly after crossing the border, we stopped for our scheduled lunch. However, given we were not that far from our destination of Prague, it was decided by the majority that we would skip lunch and travel on. That decision was a blessing in disguise, particularly for the five of us who had fallen into excess the night before.

We were staying in the large Hotel Kupa which boasted two towers, linked at the top by a sky bridge. It was 22 levels and was situated around 25 minutes from the heart of the city. Even though it was not 'five stars', it was in such stark contrast to our accommodation in

Berlin. The only similarity between the two was that that Matthew, Richard and I were again sharing a room.

I always believed that if a person is fortunate enough to get even a small insight into the life of another in a foreign land, then that person is enriched beyond description and better for the experience. I gained such an insight, albeit briefly, into the life of a local Czechoslovakian taxi driver. The taxi pulled up to the foyer of our hotel and we immediately realised that our needs hadn't been made clear when ordering the car. There were five of us who wished to visit the city that evening, but the taxi could only seat four. Despite this, the driver most cheerfully allowed the fifth passenger to ride and drove us into the city. Our money went a very long way in Czechoslovakia and we all spent the equivalent of about five Australian dollars on the ride. It was not that the fare amounted to $25, but we were pleased to give a tip, given the driver's friendly gesture at the hotel. We hardly said a word to the driver due to the language barrier, but we could sense he was a decent man from the photograph of his family proudly displayed on the dashboard of the car and another on the visor above the windscreen. The family photograph featured our driver and presumably his wife standing behind three seated children, two of which were clearly girls, the other may have been either a son or a third daughter. The quality of the photograph was rather poor as the setting also appeared to be. The whole family, despite their 'poor' appearance were happy and content in the photograph and that spoke volumes. When we motioned for our driver to keep the change, he almost cried and thought his Christmas had come early. We thought nothing more of it and proceeded to explore the city. That exploration led us to discover far more than we had anticipated and most of us left promptly after discovering that one of the nightclubs had, as one of its features, an explicit striptease by several women. After braving another two nightclubs which were fortunately a little less unsavoury, we returned to where the taxi had dropped us off and found the same driver still there waiting for us. He managed to tell us with his very limited English, "I wait, I wait." Not only was he waiting, but other taxis had also lined up, probably hoping for the same good fortune that had earlier been bestowed upon our driver. We had been rewarded by a readily available taxi and our driver rewarded with a return fare, which of course included a similar gratuity on the way back. I realised that my prosperous, democratic homeland of Australia was so very far apart from that of Czechoslovakia, measured not only by distance but also by conditions of life. From that simple experience, I developed such a respect for that kindly Czechoslovakian and an appreciation of how the world around us really was so diverse.

Once back at the hotel, the sensible thing would have been to go straight to bed, but several of us remained up for some further drinks and good company. As the hour grew even later, I took leave of my senses and of my ability to think clearly. This was, in part, fuelled by the alcohol I had consumed in concert with others, but mostly by sheer jealousy. My dear friend and former lover, Leanne, had also had one or two drinks too many. She had, in my opinion, erred in her decision to share intimate time with another of the males on tour. In what was my own error of judgment, I determined that it was necessary to intervene in those plans and began banging on the door to their room. Matthew grabbed me from behind and was uncompromising in his suggestion that I leave them alone and instead join him and some of the others back downstairs. His actions that night demonstrated to me that his friendship was genuine and unconditional. My actions demonstrated to me that as a teenager, I was susceptible to errors of judgement. It mattered not that they stemmed from an obvious retention of feelings for Leanne; the fact remained that my judgment was in error and I had to acknowledge that. I had quickly retaken possession of my senses and was acutely aware of the discovery of self that had just occurred. Although it didn't sit comfortably with me at the time, I discovered that given particular circumstances, I was just as susceptible to certain teenage foibles as the next person. That discovery was perhaps as important as any I had made during my exchange to that point.

The next day, our entire group headed into the city for a guided tour of some of the abundant wonders of Prague. No visitor to Prague does so without walking Karlův Most (Charles Bridge). There were more than a dozen bridges crossing the River Vltava which almost perfectly divides the eastern and western parts of Prague, but it was the Charles Bridge that drew the most attention. It was one of the oldest and most iconic gothic-style structures in the world and was alive with many budding entrepreneurial buskers and entertainers with acts of all manner and kind. Add to that, hundreds of tourists and several small kiosks and we found ourselves among a very crowded part of Prague. The simple, but industrious, nature of these local people had to be admired. There was nothing simple about one act, however, and a number of us had to watch on in awe as four swordsmen jousted before us. It was like something from a movie, each wearing authentic period clothing and using real swords – the clanging of the steel confirmed that authenticity. A mistake could have not only been an affront to the elaborate choreography but rather dangerous to the health and well-being of the actors. But even without buskers and other entertainers, the bridge itself was a sight to behold. At 516 metres long and almost ten metres wide, it astounded me how the bridge builders long since passed dealt with the flowing waters below, the enormous weight of the stones and the lack of modern technology with which to achieve their purpose. The entire bridge was decorated with many magnificent statues and sculptures, which I learned were in a baroque-style and had originally been erected as early as 1700. Although I did not do so accurately, I counted well over twenty-five of the statues and sculptures as I wandered from one side of the bridge to the other.

We were once again given free time after lunch. Michael, Matthew, Paulina, Allan, Richard and I decided to explore the Jewish Quarter of Prague. The history we discovered was fascinating, albeit tragic at times. The Old-New Synagogue had perhaps the most unusual facade I had ever seen, consistent with the gothic nature of many of the buildings in Prague, but still unlike any other building. Built around 1270, it was the oldest working Synagogue in all of Europe and the fact it was still used became clearly evident when people started arriving for a service. Near the Synagogue was one of the most visited places in all of Prague and with good reason. That said, I struggled with the idea that it was a 'tourist attraction' more than a sombre place of remembrance. It was the Old Jewish Cemetery, which was originally founded in 1478 and remained Europe's oldest surviving Jewish cemetery. There were literally thousands of gravestones crammed into the cemetery, but what was particularly remarkable was that the cemetery is believed to be about twelve layers deep with over 100,000 people having been buried there. I was never one to believe in spirits, ghosts or any such supernatural phenomenon, and while I didn't see any translucent beings, I did feel something as we sat amongst the thousands of gravestones. Perhaps my 'paranormal' feeling was actually very normal, manifested simply by a deep respect for the history of what I had just experienced. It seemed that I wasn't the only one who found the visit emotionally draining as we all decided to find something else to do that might lighten the mood.

The six of us made our way down to the river and hired two small row-boats from a local vendor. We didn't row very far, partly because there was not much to explore from that vantage point, partly because none of us wanted the task of actually rowing and partly because we had only hired the boats for thirty minutes, which meant there was only so far we could go anyway. We were returning to shore when Paulina fell into the dirty Vltava River. She had been reluctant to join us in the boat because she couldn't swim. Therefore, when she fell into the river and spent the first seconds splashing and thrashing about, I jumped overboard to help. To my great dismay, after grabbing hold of Paulina, I felt my feet touch the muddy riverbed only waist deep below. The water was smelly and cold, so much so that the bus driver asked that Paulina and I get a train back out to our hotel. King Bart agreed but accompanied us for good measure. Once showered and changed, we converged on the restaurant where I had an enormous appetite to satisfy. During dinner, we met another group of exchange students who were based in Germany, but on a similar tour to ours. One of them, a girl named Lauren, was actually from the Gold Coast and we spent a couple of hours together drinking and recalling scenes from home. The familiarity with scenes from home led to a familiarity with each other that in any other setting would have taken days, weeks or even months to develop. That familiarity with each other then led to the sharing of some truly intimate moments back at her room in the hotel. It was an amazing night that perfectly punctuated my memorable time in Prague.

Things really began to look up on a number of levels with our departure from Czechoslovakia. The landscape as we approached Vienna was beyond beautiful, the dinner that night was decidedly delightful and, most happily for me, I befriended a gorgeous Canadian exchange student named Nicole. On the way to Vienna, we stopped ever so briefly at the spectacular Belvedere Palace. Despite the existence of some restorative works being undertaken at the time of our visit, it was impossible not to be mesmerised by the grandeur of that Palace and its surrounding gardens and pools. There was so much to enjoy in and around the Palace, but our time was short. It was almost cruel to expect us to leave without further exploration, but the schedule was the schedule. There was a distinct opulence in Vienna, accentuated by such glorious sights as the State Opera House, the Imperial Palace, the Vienna City Hall and the lavish Spanish Riding School. A pattern started to emerge for me the more I travelled throughout Europe, and that was that I was often visiting the oldest, or one of the oldest, of its kind in the world. This was true of the Spanish Riding School. Not only did it form an integral part of Austria's cultural heritage, but the school was also the oldest riding academy in the world. It had been developing, maintaining and performing classical horsemanship for over 430 years. We were spoiled to have secured tickets and watched in awe as the horses performed as gracefully as classical dancers, aided of course by the riders who assisted the horses to honour the choreography. To watch them effortlessly prance, march and intricately weave their way across the floor to the music of the masters of classical music was to watch art come alive. An obvious feature was the faultless consistency across not only the performance but also across the decorative saddlery, the riders' costumes and the appearance of every horse. The horses were of the Lipizzaner breed, which have often been described as both a horse of battle and a horse of ballet. Having only ridden horses a dozen or so times before and having done so rather poorly at that, I was astounded by the apparent ease at which both the horses and their riders executed the routine. The highlight for me came only moments before we were to leave the school, when I saw one of the riders taking his horse back to the Imperial Stables. I wandered off the path and called out in thanks for the performance, at which time he motioned for me to go across to him. His horse was named Conversano Amata and was relatively new to the school. Conversano Amata showed much promise in the skill mastered by few horses, namely the Levade. He explained to me that the Levade was where a horse lowers his hind quarters and raises up in front, holding that position for several seconds. It was a pose that has often been depicted in paintings and sculptures of horses with either royal or military figures riding them. Quite apart from the exceptional horses, the architecture and design of the building was also amazing. The aesthetically pleasing interior of the school was almost perfectly symmetrical, with either side of the long rectangular arena featuring two levels of seating, brilliantly bordered by carved balustrades and decoratively framed arched windows which let in an abundance of natural light. The exquisite chandeliers perfectly complemented the royal feel of the building.

Of course, a visit to Vienna would not be complete without experiencing Mozart's house. While I was never a big fan of classical music, the opportunity to again feel history was not something to be discarded. The apartment on Domgasse 5 was the only one of Mozart's Viennese apartments that still existed, despite him not having lived there since 1787. It was rather grand, with four large rooms, two smaller ones and a kitchen. It had been transformed into a museum in which the life and works of the musical genius were presented in stages, corresponding to various stages of his career.

Despite having visited two of the most prominent attractions of Vienna, most of the day was actually spent casually walking around the city and even eating at McDonald's. It was interesting to see that even though some of the item names varied, the presentation of much of the menu was common to every other McDonald's restaurant I had seen. We had not been very well prepared for the sheer cost of things in Austria – from McDonald's to a souvenir stickpin, the prices were well above anything that we had been used to. I was always looking for that unique addition to my Rotary jacket, but a number of the stickpins in one store cost more than ten Australian dollars! We dined as a group that evening in a traditional Viennese eatery complete with Viennese music and cuisine. What at home would have been a themed or unique restaurant with its exposed timber beams, brick decorative arches and beer steins hanging from racks above the bar, this style of restaurant was commonplace in Vienna. The food was delightful but couldn't match the music. Three elderly men played a cello, violin and piano accordion. Each was dressed in black pants, a white shirt and a forest green vest with a single row of gold buttons down the front. They seemed to genuinely enjoy playing for us, obviously proud of both their skill and culture. I had always loved the piano accordion even though I could never play it. My Dad had one that belonged to his grandfather, but it was confined to an old timber case, brought out only for show. The one used in the restaurant was in a far superior condition, but its bellows, too, had yellowed with the passing of time. But the Viennese gentleman seemed, to me at least, to be something of a virtuoso as he played song after song, including the locally popular *Wien Bleibt Wien* (Vienna for Ever). He told us how the song was composed by an Austrian composer named Johann Schrammel in the late 1800s. I knew that we were in Vienna when I heard the song – it was just one of those typical tunes that you immediately associate with a particular place or culture. Of course, we didn't need to be told of the name or the history of one of the songs – the song that had many of us on our feet dancing and laughing. The *Chicken Dance* was immediately recognisable and many students, acting upon the several steins of beer consumed that night, joined in the atmosphere and danced away to the song. The rest clapped in raucous support.

Although we were leaving Vienna the next day, we were not leaving Austria altogether. Our destination was a small town called Villach and travelling there was like being thrust into a movie scene. The mountain landscape, bright with flowers in bloom, was reminiscent of scenes from *The Sound of Music*. Coincidentally, or perhaps by design, songs from the soundtrack of that musical were played while we were being driven through the countryside. The only way the experience could have been any more authentic was if Maria and the Von Trapp children had been riding with us, when *My Favourite Things* rang out through the speakers of the bus. Lame or not, so many of us could not resist the urge to sing along, gaze at the passing beauty and be excited by the cloudless blue sky above. It wasn't very long before our wish to be outside and experiencing the beauty in perfect weather was granted. We stopped for lunch in an extraordinarily picturesque park with long and lush green grass, flowers and even swings and monkey-bars. Lunch comprised of fresh bread rolls with several types of cold meat, juicy ripe tomatoes, lettuce and an array of fresh fruit, including succulent strawberries, crispy apples and delicious bananas. Indeed, these were just *a few of my favourite things*! As we finished lunch, a group of young local boys turned up at the park and proceeded to play football. Several of the males in our group and one of the females offered an impromptu and short game with the locals. They appeared to thoroughly enjoy making us all look very amateurish. Again, our schedule dictated that it was time to go and that probably saved us from an even more embarrassing score.

That evening, many of the exchange students became close. This, in part, was through games where coins were passed from one person to the next, using only our mouths and clothing was very much optional. Dropping the coin as it passed from one mouth to the next resulted in the loss of an item of clothing. Nicole and I left the festivities early, though, to enjoy each other's company in private and to get an early night. I sensed something very special was developing between us that night.

We literally had to drive through the Austrian mountains the next day in order to leave Austria and enter Italy. Close to the Italian border, we arrived upon numerous tunnels carved right through the mountains that were simply too high to drive over. During this drive, I was seated right at the front of the bus on the top level. In front of me was plenty of leg room and a wide windscreen that gave an uninterrupted view of the road ahead. It really was the pick of the seats and not all the students managed to get the opportunity to enjoy it over the eighteen days on tour. Nicole asked if she could sit on the floor in front of me for a while and naturally, I obliged. I began massaging her shoulders and ended up doing so for close to an hour. We talked about everything from our families, both those in Denmark and in our respective homelands, about our education before arriving in Denmark and our goals and ambitions for the future. Nicole was a beautiful girl, with very long brown hair, a cute smile and rather busty. Her sense of humour and quick wit were as appealing to me as any of her attractive physical features. We certainly became very close friends throughout the course of the tour.

We were truly spoiled with our first introduction to Italy. Lido de Jeslo, an idyllic beachside town located right on Italy's Adriatic Coast, was our first stop and was absolutely beautiful. We arrived with most of the day left and were given that remaining time to do and see what we pleased, which was a welcome break. Most of us made full use of the stunning sunny conditions by heading straight to the beach for fun in the sun. The water provided soothing respite from what was actually a very hot day and with over fifteen kilometres of beach, Lido had more than enough beach to share. For others, the attraction of Europe's longest pedestrian zone, lined with large and small retailers of all kinds, was too great to resist. For those so minded, it was off to the shops once they had re-opened after siesta. Back at the beach, I was approached by a most seedy looking character who introduced himself as the owner of a local nightclub. Once we established that English was the only language in which we could converse, he invited me back to the club to check it out. My sense of adventure was tempted by the invitation and despite warnings in Danish from my friends to be careful, I decided to accept the offer. The man had introduced himself by name, but I couldn't understand it, given how quickly he spoke. We arrived at the nightclub and it all appeared legitimate enough. Inside was a fantastic club that I could tell would be great fun when operating in the evenings. The design and layout was classy and fun with an illuminated dance floor, leather lounges around the extremities and three well-stocked bars. The owner offered me some Birra Poretti, which was an Italian beer brewed in a town called Varese, which was not far from Milan. My host told me, to the extent that I could understand, that Birra Poretti was first brewed in the late 1800s and that its founder was in some way related to him. Again, he spoke quickly and with a thick accent, so there was some information that I missed. The beer itself tasted reasonable, but it didn't come close to the good old Aussie beer, XXXX or the fantastic Grøn Tuborg from Denmark. But it was certainly cold, which on such a hot balmy day was most welcomed and easily enabled me to respond diplomatically with, "Ah, this is really good." I appreciated the concerns of my friends, but they were unwarranted. Furthermore, I was on alert the whole time and took nothing for granted. My new-found Italian friend thanked me for visiting and gave me free passes for all the exchange students on the tour. I took great delight in distributing them to my friends for use later that evening. As it turned out, we never actually returned to the club, which was disappointing. The alternative mischief that a select few of us found ourselves in outweighed any initial disappointment though.

The 'select few' was, more accurately, about thirty of us, of which only a handful were male. Again, with only 15 of the 54 students on tour being male, that ratio was not surprising. After having enjoyed some drinks and companionship in the rooms of our hotel, the 'select few' decided to go down to the beach. Once there, most of us abandoned our inhibitions and our clothes and ran naked into the cooling waters of the Adriatic Sea. It was quite late, but still very warm and the water very inviting. We splashed around in a display of youthful exuberance for about half an hour before retiring back to the hotel. There had been no harm done whatsoever, but upon our return to the hotel, our reception was colder than the water in which we had just been swimming. The manager of the hotel believed she was accommodating a bus full of Rotarians, not Rotary exchange students. The Hotel Oceanic was a nice hotel. Still not the Ritz or Sheraton, but it was exceedingly classier than the hostel we stayed at in Berlin. When some thirty wet, sandy students returned from their late-night beach bonanza, the manager took great umbrage at the fact and shut off the hot water to our rooms. Not only that, but she had confiscated our towels, so the bed sheets served two purposes that evening. It was impossible to go to bed sticky from the salt water and sandy from the beach itself, so it was cold showers all round. Although, given the cleaning of the beds that would have been required the next day, many thought it would have been worth going to bed sandy in retaliation.

The following morning, Nicole and I almost missed breakfast. It was fortunate that we didn't as we needed all the energy possible to survive the long day trip to Venice and back again. Our trusty Tjæreborg bus could only take us so far on our expedition to Venice before we all boarded a boat bound for the heart of the canal city. St. Mark's

Square was our central meeting point and perhaps one of the most famous landmarks in Venice. Of course, it was famous for the historic and impressive architecture of the buildings surrounding the square, but also for the thousands of pigeons that call the square home. The pigeon population in Venice and, predominantly, St. Mark's Square was actually greater than that of the entire human population of Venice. One brochure I read suggested that there were over 100,000 pigeons in and around the square. Beyond the obvious damage to the buildings caused by the pigeon droppings, I was interested to learn that the pigeons, like chickens, seek out sources of calcium carbonate for their eggs. This in turn resulted in the pigeons pecking at the most exposed parts of the marble on and around the buildings in Venice, as well as at the stucco that had previously been used in restorative works. There was much to see and do in Venice and we were largely left on our own to do so.

The Doge Palace which faces onto both the Venetian Lagoon and St Mark's Square was perhaps one of the most well-known sights in Venice. Of course, closely associated with that was the famous Bridge of Sighs. The bridge crossed over the Rio di Palazzo, connecting the Doge Palace to the old prison. It was colloquially called the Bridge of Sighs because it was the last view of Venice that prisoners would get passing through the enclosed bridge and it was said that they would 'sigh' at their final view of the outside world. I doubted that there was much to actually see through the windows of the bridge as they were covered by stone grills. I had to pause at the windows to see anything but light shine through. I couldn't fault the romantic history though and was happy to accept the etymology of the name. Of course, part of that romantic history had been advanced over centuries by the tales of the legendary Casanova. Known as an unrepentant womaniser, Casanova accrued a long list of blasphemies, seductions, fights and public controversies before being imprisoned. He was apparently the only one to have passed through the Bridge of Sighs, be imprisoned and escape. He was also a prolific writer and traveller who associated with European Royalty, Popes, Cardinals and such luminaries as Voltaire and Mozart. Whatever the accurate record of his life may have been, his name certainly remained synonymous with 'womanising'.

The more romantic foundation for the naming of the Bridge of Sighs was that if couples kissed on a gondola at sunset under the bridge, they would sigh and be assured of eternal love. Our itinerary didn't permit Nicole and me to remain in the canal city until sunset to test that more romantic theory. Apart from the rich legend attached to the bridge, it was of itself a rather impressive architectural structure. Constructed of limestone, the external finishing of the bridge featured intricate and elaborate carvings and sculptures, making it irresistible for the ever-increasing number of people who photographed it daily.

The highlight of Venice though, was not the prodigious pigeon population, nor the romantic canals and buildings. It was the lunch that five of us enjoyed in a small traditional Italian restaurant right on the water's edge. Tucked away on an inauspicious canal not far from St. Mark's Square, the little 'ristorante' was a real treat. We had chosen the restaurant purely on the recommendation of our gondola boatman and would not have otherwise found it without his guidance. To my limited knowledge of Italian restaurants, this appeared quite classically styled with a serene dining room and quaint little wine bar at the rear. Although small, it had exposed beam ceilings and one wall was entirely dedicated to the shelving of a wide array of wines. We pooled our lunch money and together ordered pizza and lasagne. It is difficult to describe terrific taste at the best of times, much less than when the food was so exquisite. I had never experienced a lasagne alla bolognese so perfect in every way.

Often a lasagne will have a lovely crispy top, but collapse under the pressure of a knife, or be so dry that layers of leather make for a better description. This lasagne had a lovely golden-brown cheese-baked crust, yet the knife simply fell through the remaining meat filled layers of pasta with the ease of a razor. It did take a little while to serve after ordering and I guessed that it must have been because of its traditional preparation in stages. Eating there had certainly been a treat, and we were grateful for having found the restaurant. The only down-side to the wonderful lunch was that we had virtually used all our spare time and had to move very quickly to get back to St. Mark's Square to rendezvous with the rest of the group.

If our day in Venice had been busy, then our trip the next day to Diano Marina was hectic beyond measure. Not only were there some 600 kilometres to travel, but also sights to see along the way. The most notable of these sights was the town of Verona, about 200 kilometres from our beachside retreat at Lido. Verona was perhaps most famous for being the home of the characters in the Shakespearean tragedy, Romeo and Juliet. Verona was also home to an ancient arena, second only in size to that of the great colosseum in Rome and was at the time of our visit under repair. The 'Arena di Verona' was a Roman amphitheatre with origins dating back to the year 30 AD. Despite the crumbling stone columns and arches, we were still able to enter the arena and sit among the rows of concrete seating and imagine what it must have been like to be spectators in ancient times. The arena was memorable, impressive even, but the highlight of Verona for me had to be Juliet's Balcony. As a student in Australia, I had read Shakespeare and was familiar with the tragedy of Romeo and Juliet. One can look at photographs or conjure mental images of features from literature, but to stand before that which has been read about and studied was to stand in awe. Juliet's Balcony in Verona was truly a sight to see, elevated high above the bronze statuette of Juliet in the cobblestone forecourt. The experience was made even more special by the fact that my own 'Juliet' was able to stand on the balcony and wave down to me. Nicole and I were becoming very close indeed.

Despite the very full schedule that day, we managed a late swim at the beach in Diano Marina on our arrival. As was the case in Lido de Jesolo, the weather was fine and hot – the perfect combination for swimming. Dinner was at 8:00pm, but Nicole and I showered together for over an hour after returning from the beach and managed to miss dinner altogether. Our burgeoning romance became the topic of conversation over the next couple of days.

Heavenly is perhaps the only way to describe our final day in Italy. We were still in Diano Marina and our schedule was entirely free to do whatever it was we desired. Some slept, as sleep had been something most of us had neglected to do for most of the tour. Others again enjoyed the soothing waters of the ocean. Only this time, the 'ocean' was the glorious Ligurian Sea, which was an arm of the mighty Mediterranean Sea further to the west. The boundaries of the Ligurian Sea were effectively the Italian Riviera and the island of Corsica, but also touched the shores of France and Monaco. The bravest of the group added some local exploration to their day, with idyllic views from the nearby hills proving very much the spectacular photo opportunity. A handful of forward-thinking students took the opportunity to wash some of their clothes. I was one of those who had to do some washing, although it was not of free choice. I had purchased a lovely bottle of red wine in Venice for Bendt and Clara, but to my great dismay, it had smashed in my suitcase and soaked most of my clothes. Once the domestic chores were out of the way, I joined Nicole for a short wander through the small town before surrendering to the allure of the sea once more. In a most strange sensation, for the first time on exchange, some of us got some colour from the stunningly warm summer sun. It was perhaps the most relaxing afternoon I had ever had.

Leaving Italy saw us pass briefly through Monaco on our heading to the southern regions of France. Little can be said about the obvious opulence that Monaco and its people exhibit, beyond that it was entirely conspicuous. Multi-million-dollar vessels moored at exclusive yacht clubs surrounded by some of the world's most expensive real estate occupied most views around the city. Apartment towers, complete with extensive rooftop gardens and pools were also in abundance. In the western part of Monaco, we visited the Place du Palais. As far as palaces went and given how elaborate everything else in Monaco appeared to be, it wasn't that spectacular. In fairness, it had originally been built centuries earlier not as a palace, but as a fortress. What was impressive was the bald rocky outcrop of mountain that formed an imposing backdrop to the palace. At that height, the view back over Monte Carlo was as breathtaking as the sheer wealth represented by the images within that view below. The beautiful landmark that was the Cathédrale de Monaco (Monaco Cathedral), was a must-see destination. Thousands of fans of the actress Grace Kelly, who – famously and in fairy-tale fashion – became the Princess of Monaco after marrying her husband Prince Rainier III, would visit the landmark annually. In further tribute to Princess Grace, was the pulchritudinous Princess Grace Rose Garden, in full colour during our short visit. Of course, no visit to Monaco would be complete without at least setting eyes upon the famous Monte-Carlo Casino. Built in 1863, its intricate architecture and splendorous interior design were simply brilliant. Although I was old enough, I certainly lacked anywhere near the money, time or attire to venture beyond the front steps of the truly grand attraction.

We arrived at Avignon in the southernmost part of France. I felt fortunate to have visited both the very northern regions of France at Easter and, with our arrival in Avignon, the very southern regions of the same country. One significant difference, of course, was that my visit to the north had included snow and tobogganing. On arriving in Avignon, the mercury hit almost 42 degrees Celsius, so instead of snow, there was sweat. Actually, a couple of the students suffered blood noses from the very hot conditions.

Just outside of Avignon was an enormous legacy of the Romans. I had seen the work of the Romans before, but this surpassed anything I had seen. Their renowned penchant for quality and greatness was evident in the edifice that stood in silent solitude before me. The Pont du Gard, an ancient aqueduct, simply inspired awe. To the extent that an inanimate object can be, this magnificent piece of ancient infrastructure was somewhat intimidating. We were informed that the difference in the level between either end of the aqueduct produced a gradient of some 24 millimetres per metre. That for me, made the impressive structure even more impressive. I had to wonder how, in the middle of nowhere, the Romans, in times before Christ, were able to so meticulously construct such a megastructure. We were also told how the Pont du Gard was added to the United Nations Educational, Scientific and Cultural Organisation (UNESCO) list of World Heritage Sites in 1985. Its inclusion on that list could not be questioned – it deserved the protection and preservation provided for under the World Heritage Convention.

Back at our hostel and despite the sun having gone down, the temperature had hardly relented. This was made even more unbearable by the terrible, almost non-existent circulation of air in what were really small rooms. Furthermore, the rather hostile hostel manager patrolled the rooms, ensuring no alcohol was being consumed. As a result, and almost without exception, the vast majority of students headed to the river's edge where the slightest of breezes coming off the river marginally dropped the temperature. The rush to shower, pack and eat breakfast before our early departure was quite the calamity. With some encouragement from our guide and from the rest of us, the handful of particularly 'slower-to-start' students were finally ready.

Avignon to Paris saw Nicole and I enjoy each other's company on the bus for the long haul, which took a little over seven hours to drive. Even though we were travelling at close quarters with so many other students, Nicole and I were often intensely close throughout the trip. We were oblivious to our confined surroundings for much of the 600 kilometre or so drive to Paris. We made a couple of stops, one scheduled and one not. The scheduled stop was for the necessities of life – food and water. We discovered that the toilet facilities at the small road-side stop were less appealing than those on the bus – especially for the girls who weren't as well equipped to 'aim' at a recessed floor drain as the males were. Our second and unscheduled stop was at the behest of a French police officer who had taken umbrage at something that our driver had done – I never found out what that was. As uncomfortable and monotonous as those hours in hot conditions were, they were entirely worth it when we started to see the romantic city rise mystically from the horizon. Sharply accenting that wondrous view was the sight of the Eiffel Tower reaching far into the airy heights above Paris. It was really a most defining attraction and proved to be a very useful landmark when navigating the city. Our lodgings for the three-day, two-night stay in Paris were located in an old inner city building that had weathered many long years. Despite its appearance, it was charming and surprisingly comfortable. The manager though, like some earlier in the trip, was a little less charming when insisting no alcohol be taken into, much less consumed in, the rooms.

Our itinerary for Paris was very full and required long days to complete. Fortunately, the next morning, we were spoiled with cereal, toast, jam, croissants, baguettes and fruit, which, compared to some of our breakfasts on tour, was a veritable banquet. Such sustenance was needed though, as early that morning, we all boarded the bus for a general familiarisation tour of the city and its attractions. We were joined by a tall, young French guide, named Alexander. His thorough knowledge of the city and its many attractions was welcomed as we all devised our own mini-itineraries during the orientation tour. We took in the Louvre, the Arc de Triomphe, the Cathedral Notre Dame and of course, the Eiffel Tower. Around lunchtime, we were set free on the streets of Paris. Nicole and I ventured to yet another McDonald's restaurant, not necessarily for the dietary preference, but mostly because all the quaint and traditional French cafes and eateries were shockingly expensive – at least for an exchange student's budget. Straight from lunch, Nicole and I walked to one of the world's most recognisable tourist attractions – the Eiffel Tower. After sharing a kiss with Nicole under the very centre of the Tower, we paid the 51

French Franc and took the elevator to the summit, stopping at each of the levels on the way up. I had never really been afraid of heights, nor of elevators, but the ride up the Eiffel Tower had my nerves on edge. It was not so much the height, although that was indeed great, but the rickety clanging of the wire mesh cage as it made its way up the structure. My postural equilibrium certainly felt challenged. I had read in brochures beforehand, that the tower had originally only been designed to last twenty years, which left me feeling slightly uncomfortable. Here we were, more than 100 years after it had been built, making the pilgrimage that millions before us had made. Of course, I was quick to remind myself that it was regularly maintained, which had given it a life more than five times that which was originally intended. As nerve-racking as it may have been, I couldn't let Nicole notice. What's more, irrespective of the feeling on the way up, arriving at the top of that French masterpiece more than adequately compensated. Perhaps only soaring eagles could have enjoyed a finer view of that famously romantic city, on what was a most delightful day. Every sensation seemed more intense – the view stimulated my sight more than almost anything had before, the sound of what was a light and pleasant breeze seemed louder at that height and, while not an immediately recognisable physiological 'sense', the feelings for Nicole were equally heightened.

We could have spent longer up, on and around the Tower, but in a recurring theme of our tour, time was at a premium. Nicole and I resolved to give our feet a rest and boarded a Seine River cruise boat, the port for which was only metres away. Just adjacent to the bridge named Pont d'Iena, was the port known as Port de la Bourdonnais and was the perfect place to start our Seine River experience. A boat was almost immediately available, with the wait being little more than a few minutes. It was a narrow, but very long boat with about half of its length covered by a roof, the rear had an open-air deck with rows upon rows of seats. It was serene and like something from a romance movie, which was appropriate given the way Nicole and I felt for each other. It wasn't a long cruise though, as we were getting off little more than four or five kilometres down river. We disembarked at the oldest bridge in Paris, the Pont Neuf, from where it was only a short walk to the Cathedral Notre Dame. We wanted a closer inspection of that gothic religious icon of Paris, of film and of literature, which had not been possible as the bus passed it earlier in the day on our orientation tour.

Much could be written about why I was so impressed with that cathedral. I learned that the 'flying buttress' element of the construction evolved in the Gothic era of architecture. Apparently, this helped buildings – often churches – be built taller and more narrowly. Beyond the architecture was the incredible and ornate lead-light glass throughout. Some of these elements are common to many buildings around Europe. It never ceased to amaze me though, how among the similarities, each had something uniquely awe-inspiring about them.

Almost 20 minutes away was the equally famous Louvre Museum. Nicole had an eye for art, so it was hardly surprising that we included that in our itinerary for the day. I was, of course, enormously grateful that I had the experience of visiting the Louvre, but felt at the same time that it was one of the few sights of Paris I would not need to see again.

While it was already getting late in the afternoon, Nicole and I could not resist the temptation to take a walk along at least part of what had been called the most beautiful avenue in the world – the Avenue des Champs-Élysées. The perfectly maintained chestnut trees, decoratively paved footpaths, cafes and luxury specialty shops that made it one of the most expensive strips of real estate in the world was certainly worth the hike. Although Nicole and I couldn't afford any trinkets from any of the stores along the strip – even if we had combined our resources – it was the fact that we had experienced it that was special. Dinner that night was in a small French eatery called Le Diamant Bleu. It must be said that we generally ate very well in Paris, although at times the cultural influence on the menu made some of the dishes hard to stomach. I ordered a well-done steak and upon receiving it at my table, initially thought that language had let me down when ordering. I considered the steak rare, or medium-rare at best, but after discussing it with the waiter, it became obvious that he considered my steak well-done and most acceptable. I was sickened to think what a steak ordered rare might look like but did manage to eat mine as served. I didn't notice right at that moment, but it became clear to me over the course of my exchange that my tastes were maturing with every new culinary experience that challenged my otherwise unadventurous palate.

We were exhausted from our first full day in Paris, but that proved to be only a precursor for a bigger, busier and fuller day two. It started even earlier, so our breakfast, while still satisfying, was very rushed. We then boarded the bus and headed directly to the most spectacular palace I had ever seen.

Unlike the Place du Palais in Monaco, the Palace of Versailles was a palace to behold. The sheer beauty and grandeur of the Palace and its gardens was so striking, that even angels in flight would surely stop to gaze in awe. The grand gates adorned with gold were only a sample of what lay in waiting for us inside.

Entire passages could be written on virtually every aspect of the Palace. Its many special rooms, chambers and salons each had a rich and unique history, surpassed only by an abundant splendour of gold, silk, marble and other interior features that defy description. In the French monarchy, the King was said to be chosen by God, and through coronation, be his 'lieutenant on earth'. Because of this, the Palace housed an elaborate and expansive chapel. Ornately carved pillars and arches accentuated the interior of the chapel, with religious paintings and sculptures evoking that notion of the King being chosen by God. For me though, the most resplendent evidence of opulence within the Palace was the famous 'Hall of Mirrors'. The use of gold, crystal and marble was astounding, but it was the 350 or so mirrors that decorated the seventeen arches opposite the grand windows that so defined the feature. The very feeling of royalty manifested itself within me as I took one long and envious stroll through the Hall of Mirrors.

As brilliant as the Palace and its thousands of internal features were, my breath was most taken by the enormity and magnificence of the gardens. Not dissimilar to the Palace, the gardens had so many aspects to them and were far too vast to explore. Nicole and I literally had to run around to see as much as we did. There were more than ten fountains alone, but the Latona Fountain and the Apollo Fountain were sights to behold. The first illustrated the legend of Apollo's mother protecting her children from peasants, while the Apollo Fountain depicted the mighty Apollo driving his chariot behind noble horses. The use of marble and gilded lead in the creation of these fountains was extraordinary, especially given the craftsmanship on both dated back to the 1600s. Water was a very noticeable feature of the gardens. In what appeared to be basically a prolongation of the facade of the Palace, there were two massive rectangular ornamental pools immediately outside. The information brochures informed us that the pools were designed to reflect sunlight up the facade of the Palace and into the Hall of Mirrors. Each of the two pools had four statues that symbolised the rivers of France, namely the Loire, the Loiret, the Rhône, the Saône, the Seine, the Marne, the Garaonne and the Dordogne. I marvelled at the fact that not only in the forecourt and elsewhere at the amazing Palace of Versailles, but in many places I had visited in Europe, the decorations, sculptures, statues and other such ornaments all told stories or represented some aspect of history or legend. They were permanent reminders of times long ago but remained modern-day story tellers at the same time. In keeping with the extensive use of water throughout the gardens, the Grand Canal was a most defining feature. Extending more than 1500 metres in length, the picturesque water feature was once home to various nautical pursuits and further exemplified the importance of water and the light it reflected.

But in perhaps the most poignant display of the lengths the early French royalty would go to in order to achieve grandeur was the Orangerie. This was simply a vast open space – so vast that it would be measured in hectares – filled with sections of neatly kept lawn, a circular pond and in summer, as it was when we were there, over 1000 trees. The trees were a variety of species, from palms to oleanders, pomegranates and orange, with some of them being over two hundred years old.

That excursion into the extraordinary occupied the first few hours of the day and, given how early we had started, meant that we still had most of the day free to do whatever we pleased. A few of the exchange students decided to venture well outside the city limits to Euro Disneyland. Although out of the city limits and involving a 'special fare' zone on the train, it was only about 35 minutes from the city to within a short walk of the front gates. There were only six of us who felt the experience would be worthwhile and only six of us who could add the awesome adventure to the pages of our diaries. Nicole and I were among them, joined by Annalise, Paulina, Chad and Allan. Euro Disneyland was still a very young attraction in France and on our visit, had very few patrons. So young was the park, it had only opened the month before we arrived. There were still some copies of the 'official opening' brochures around the park and an extract of the official dedication by the Chief Executive Officer of the Walt Disney Company was included. It read:

> To all who come to this happy place, welcome. Once upon a time...A master storyteller, Walt Disney, inspired by Europe's best loved tales, used his own special gifts to share them with the world. He envisioned a Magic Kingdom where these stories would come to life and called it Disneyland. Now his dream returns to the lands that inspired it. Euro Disneyland is dedicated to the young and the young at heart...with a hope that it will be a source of joy and inspiration for all the world. Michael D. Eisner, 12 April 1992.

It most certainly was a 'Magic Kingdom' and was most definitely 'a source of joy and inspiration' for all of us. Also, the fact there were so few patrons visiting that day was to our great advantage. We didn't wait for one single ride or show, and we were able to sample everything the enormous park had to offer, from the 'Adams Family House' to 'The Paddle Steamer – Mark Twain'. I showed my prowess in the shooting gallery, hitting 49 of the 50 available targets, before joining the five others in and on so many other attractions at the park. On a site just beside Euro Disneyland was another themed attraction called 'The Streets of America'. Walking through 'The Streets of America' was just like doing that very thing. We had, in our illustrious group of six, two Americans and a Canadian, so the authenticity of the attraction was easily validated. It was extremely late when we returned on the train to Paris. We had missed the scheduled dinner at 'Le Diamant Bleu' by many hours, so Nicole and I enjoyed pizza at a restaurant only minutes from the Eiffel Tower. After dinner, the two of us took a lovely walk through the nearby park and found ourselves again at the foot of the famous French landmark. It had been said that Paris was a city of romance and as we stood there, Nicole and I certainly felt that to be true, as we enjoyed the final attraction of the day – each other.

Our third day in Paris was also the day we were to leave, and we only had time for one final hearty breakfast before heading to Brussels. After the trip from Avignon to Paris, we were certainly no strangers to long road trips, and Paris to Brussels was another such drive. We had little time in Brussels, but enough to see the famous Manneken Pis peeing cheekily into the pond below his pedestal. The Manneken Pis was to Brussels as the Statue of Liberty was to New York or The Little Mermaid statue was to Copenhagen.

Despite only standing about sixty centimetres tall, the little bronze statue was a major tourist attraction. Even though its existence could be dated back to the early 1600s, the origins of the little Manneken remained the source of many divergent stories. Our guide told us several stories, including that a little boy had relieved himself against the door of a witch who lived where the fountain now stood. She was so angry at his doing so, that she turned him into a bronzed statue. Another was that during the 14th Century, Brussels was being attacked by a foreign power. The enemies had placed explosive charges at the city walls, but a small local boy had witnessed them do so. He was said to have urinated on the burning fuse and as a result, saved the city. Perhaps the story that seemed most realistic was that in which a wealthy merchant lost his son during a visit to the city. The merchant put together a search party and searched the city only to find his little boy happily peeing in a small garden. In an expression of thanks to the local citizens who helped him find his son, the merchant had the fountain built with a small statue to represent his little son urinating when found. Irrespective of which story made the most sense, it was enjoyable listening to all of them. Unlike many tourists who see the little Manneken 'naked', we had the privilege of seeing him dressed.

There was a jazz festival planned for the weekend in Brussels, so the cheeky little Manneken was dressed up in a white jazz outfit, complete with little white shoes and a hat. He was rather talented, because in addition to doing what it is he is famous for, he was also able to hold a little silver and gold saxophone. I asked our guide whether the Manneken was dressed very often and to my surprise, he told us that the City Museum housed more than 600 different costumes that the bronzed, but incontinent, little statue had worn in the past.

Like so many parts of Europe, several of which we had already seen, The Grand-Place in Brussels was another UNESCO protected World Heritage Site. It occurred to me, that in a relatively short time, I had seen so many of these understandably protected sites. In my youth, I had visited over a dozen of the UNESCO World Heritage Sites when travelling Australia with my family. There I was, almost a decade later, visiting many of Europe's fine examples of such protected sites. A very large square, some 110 metres long, The Grand-Place was very crowded with performance stages, seating and hundreds of people. It was an extraordinarily homogeneous collection of buildings and was very much alive with the sights and sounds of those preparing for the weekend jazz festival.

As a person who always took pride in who they were and where they had come from, it was not surprising that the history of the Grand-Place resonated with me. I learned that the French troops of Louis XIV destroyed the Grand-Place in just three days in 1695. When rebuilding the site, the Brussels bourgeoisie were determined to restore it to its former glory, rather than build it to some contemporary style. I left the Grand-Place and Brussels with a deep respect for the pride the local Belgians obviously had for their home all those centuries earlier.

We continued from Brussels to Elst, which was where we were to spend our last night in a bed. The next night would be spent on the lengthy drive back to Denmark. Elst was a reasonably small village to the south-east of Amsterdam, famous for its Roman temples located under the Saint Werenfried Church in the centre of town. We were staying in the countryside just outside of town where there was virtually nothing but our youth hostel, a bar and a few shops on the main road. We were almost two hour's drive from anywhere, but still managed to party heartily into the early hours of the morning. This was aided by the fact that the barman was named Bart – which coincidentally was the nickname of our guide – which left all involved, including the two Barts, rather amused. At one point, Matthew, Paulina, Nicole and I ventured out into a small wood nearby, where we were surprised to see some deer grazing in the wild. Unfortunately, our presence scared them away before we could return with our cameras. The fact that we were probably just a little loud didn't help our cause with the deer. Given that it was the final night on tour in which we would enjoy a bed, Nicole decided to share hers with me. It was slightly cramped, but we both woke feeling suitably rested.

Just as Elst had been our final night in accommodation, Saturday, 23 May 1992 saw us visit our final destination on tour – Amsterdam. There was much to see in a short time and it was therefore necessary to prioritise that which we particularly wished to see. The students, as they had done many times before on tour, split up and went their own way. There were numerous museums, exhibiting everything from art to sex, and while the latter may have been interesting, time just did not allow it. Instead, my group visited the Van Gogh Museum and the House of Anne Frank. The Van Gogh Museum featured the largest exhibition of Vincent Van Gogh's work in the world and was as unique as it was extensive. I had never been a connoisseur of art, but the sheer volume of quality work was such that I didn't need to be to appreciate Van Gogh's decades of artistic pursuit.

As with Juliet's Balcony in Verona, the House of Anne Frank enabled me to see that which I had previously studied. That was, again, a genuinely satisfying experience. No matter how great a regard I already had for Anne Frank and her diarised struggle, it was heightened by visiting her house and seeing for myself the cramped conditions in which she and her family lived in hiding during those difficult years of the war. Trying to imagine myself in those incommodious lodgings was painful enough – the thought of having to actually live in them drew such posthumous empathy and compassion for Anne and her family, that tears welled in my eyes. Add to that the fact that Anne and her family were discovered, arrested and transported to concentration camps after enduring for so long, was almost enough to make me cry. The premises at 263 Prinsengracht in Amsterdam had been maintained with remarkable authenticity as a continuing reminder of the tragedy that was recorded in the pages of Anne's diary. Even the markings on the wall that evidenced the physical growth of Anne and her sister Margo were preserved. The first line marked on the wall was made on 18 September 1942, when Anne was just thirteen years of age and 155 centimetres tall. Another marking was made on her first birthday in hiding, the 12th of June 1943 and the last a little over a year later, just before they were discovered. At that time, Anne was 168 centimetres tall, evidencing that she had grown thirteen centimetres during her time in hiding. That visit for me, was unquestionably the highlight of my visit to Amsterdam and among my top five for the entire trip. There were of course, other 'lights' that drew much attention – all red. Amsterdam's famous red-light district was certainly an eye-opener and for obvious reasons around safety and propriety, was only briefly explored.

Our final dinner was memorable for all manner of reasons. A number of exchange students were celebrating their birthdays either that day or not long after, it was the last night we were all to sit down to dinner as a group, and it was an Indonesian menu. As a group, we purchased souvenir T-shirts for the students enjoying their birthdays together with some wine and chocolate for Queen Pee Pee (Pernille), King Bart (Carsten) and our drivers. I was truly astonished at the choice of restaurant, given that many of us had delicate sensitivities when it came to food. Our table must have consumed ten jugs of water as we tried to feast our way through the banquet style dinner. I had burning lips for hours after the food had passed through them. Our guides will certainly think twice before taking fifty-four exchange students to an Indonesian restaurant again, especially on the night of such a long and confined drive on a bus. That lengthy overnight drive back to Denmark was not without a distinct odour, reminiscent of what was eaten at dinner.

We departed Amsterdam at about 11:00pm and headed directly home to Denmark. Most of the students started to wake around 6:00am and about one hour later, we stopped at the border between Germany and Denmark for breakfast. After breakfast, all 54 exchange students lined up their cameras, and Pernille, Carsten and our driver all shared the task of taking a group photograph of us standing or sitting in front of the yellow bus that had so reliably transported us throughout Europe. In fact, during our extraordinary travels around

Europe, the bus had added well over five thousand kilometres to its odometer.

Over the eighteen days on tour, the exchange students and our guides bonded with each other to an extent truly beyond description. Sure, we had participated in all kinds of mischief and fun, but we also had our horizons broadened with knowledge and experience. More and more seats were being vacated, as the bus weaved its way northward through Danish towns like a thread in tapestry. At every stop, there were tears, cuddles and promises of letters and phone calls. Importantly, there was also an abundance of laughter and satisfaction in the knowledge that we had all just experienced something phenomenal.

Within about three weeks of the Euro-Tour ending, we all received the Euro-Tour 1992 diary that we had contributed to during the tour. This had been the brainchild of Pernille and Carsten, so it was only appropriate that they wrote the final words within the diary:

> *Well, here it is, the 1992 Euro-Tour Diary. We hope that it will be able to bring back memories in the years to come. For us it will, that's for sure! We really hope that we were able to make you guys enjoy this Euro-Tour, just as much as we did. A lot of things had to work out, to make it a successful tour – the weather, the few rules, the driver, the food, the guides and last but not least, yourselves! Everything seemed to work out so well, so there's no doubt – you're the best! With Love, Pernille and Carsten.*

6

Family Two

Carl and Marie were lovely people. Carl was the principal of a real estate agency in Højberg and from all accounts was well respected among not only his many satisfied clients, but his colleagues as well. He was about my height and, behind his large round glasses, had kind eyes. Marie was essentially a homemaker, although had many interests outside the home. She immediately felt like a long-lost relative to me. Her short hair was blonde and her demeanour so very welcoming. Neither had the command of the English language that Clara and Bendt had, but I saw that only to my advantage as I continued to learn Danish. Marie was openly anxious about speaking English. Such was her concern, she had only recently completed a refresher course in English before I arrived. I did my best to assure Marie that between her English and my increasing Danish, we would be just fine. I was very touched that she would go to that effort just for me. They had two children, Mikkel and Johanna, although it was only Johanna who lived at home. Mikkel was several years older than me and had been living with his girlfriend for some time in an apartment of his own in the city. Johanna was much younger than me and was quite shy at first, in part because her English was in its early stages of development. The final member of the family was Mille. Mille was a beautiful West Highland Terrier and was affectionately called 'Lille Mille'. Lille, the

Danish word for little, rhymed with Mille and was rather cute to use in conjunction with Mille's name. Mille had the most curious habit in that she would come running from anywhere if she heard the word 'ost' – which is the Danish word for cheese.

Carl and Marie's home was very comfortable with ample living space. It had originally been built with an indoor swimming pool, but through lack of use, they had decided to convert it into an additional living room. The empty pool still existed below the floor and was discreetly used for storage purposes. If one were to jump on the floor however, the echo easily gave away the existence of the void below.

Time was always my enemy in Denmark, but this was particularly so with my wonderful second host family. The months I were to spend with Carl, Marie and Johanna were entirely summer months and as a result, there was so much to do. It was unfortunate that I had to settle in with Carl and Marie, only to inform them that I had previously made travel plans. Matthew and I had planned to spend ten days in England with a couple who were good friends with his parents. However, our departure date fell only two weeks after I moved into my second host home. Those two weeks, although only short, proved more than sufficient for me to become very comfortable and at ease with my new host family. Importantly, I felt as though it had been enough time for them to feel the same way about me. Another special connection was well and truly being made.

As much as time is a valuable commodity, its value is enhanced if wisely spent. This was the way I approached my time with Carl and Marie. Given the demands on my time, it was paramount that the time I did have with them was well spent and meaningful. Carl and Marie made this easy to achieve as we did a lot of activities together as a family. Golf was certainly not my forte yet was very much the sporting love for both Carl and Marie. Carl was actually the president of the prestigious Aarhus Golf Club and enjoyed regular rounds at that course. Unlike my city at home, Aarhus didn't boast numerous golf clubs and as a result, the Aarhus Golf Club was enormously popular.

Located in close proximity to the sprawling Fløjstrup Skov – a large forest right on the shores of Aarhus Bay – the golf course shared the abundant natural beauty of that neighbouring landmark. The rolling green hills, natural ponds and pockets of virgin forests combined to ensure a course that was as challenging as it was beautiful. So profound was Carl and Marie's affinity with the game, they also owned a quaint A-framed cottage at HimmerLand. HimmerLand was an exclusive golf and country club resort located just over 110 kilometres to the north of Aarhus. It offered three different eighteen-hole courses of varying difficulty and a putting green near the clubhouse. In addition, it offered club house facilities which included snooker tables, a swimming pool, spa, sauna and a restaurant and bar.

My first visit to HimmerLand came just two days after my return from England and was only for a long weekend – we left on a Friday and returned on the Sunday. HimmerLand was a little under two hours north from Aarhus, although the rolling green landscapes and traditional Scandinavian villages along the way made it a most interesting drive. It was perhaps not as interesting for Carl, Marie and Johanna, as they had made the trip many times before, but I found it most enjoyable.

Carl was actually scheduled to play in a tournament that weekend, which was primarily why we made the trip. Once there, it wasn't long before we all made the discovery that I couldn't play golf. I had never played the game before in my life and trying to do so was as foreign to me as Denmark had been all those months earlier. Fortunately, not only was Carl very skilled at playing the game, he also proved to be a passionate and patient coach. Of course, he could not work miracles and my first few games were rather embarrassing! While embarrassing at times, I was grateful that my immersion in golf was, by implication, an immersion in Carl and Marie's wonderful family. It was becoming very clear, very quickly, that I had landed a 'hole-in-one' in terms of being placed with them.

It was also during our time at HimmerLand that I got to witness a new chapter in Denmark's rich history – namely, the Danish national football team challenge for the European Championships. Denmark's involvement in the 1992 European Championships was historic for many reasons – least of which was the glorious and very much unexpected win. They were not even supposed to be in the Championships as they had replaced Yugoslavia as a qualifier after that country fell into civil war. In fact, several of the Danish players were on their summer holidays and had to be recalled. In what was perhaps one of sport's greatest underdog performances of all time, the Danish team found itself in the finals. They had drawn with football powerhouse England and had defeated France in their Group 1 games. Even the most optimistic of Danish supporters still didn't dare to believe their team could take the Championship. Then they met the defending European Champions, the Netherlands, in the semi-final. Football fans the entire continent over were shocked beyond belief when Denmark defeated the Netherlands. The win was thanks, in large part, to Danish goalkeeper Peter Schmeichel saving Marco van Basten's penalty in the final penalty shoot-out. After those wins, thoughts and dreams for victory in the competition started to infiltrate the minds of the Danes and indeed, my mind. Throughout the competition, many Danes reminded me of the enormity of the task facing the Danish team and most commentators gave them virtually no chance of winning. But while the hope of winning was almost unspeakable, there they were in the final – having already won games they apparently could not win. Germany were favourites to an extent which had rarely, if ever, been seen in the history of the Championships.

I had always seen myself and my countrymen as patriotic, intensely proud of being Australian and especially so during times of international competition. Never though, had I seen virtually an entire nation so wholesomely unified in their patriotism. Cafes and bars were overflowing and even the streets and squares around the country were packed to the point of suffocating immobility. The supporters were all dressed in red and white, painted red and white and carrying anything that was red and white. The scenes were not unlike an army as the red and white regiments rallied throughout the entire country, strategically positioning themselves ready to support their team to the very end. The result would forevermore be proudly entrenched in Danish sporting folklore. Denmark defeated the much-fancied Germany by two goals to nil.

The official anthem for the tournament was *More than a Game* and I could sense among family and friends in Denmark that the anthem was particularly relevant and meaningful to Denmark in the circumstances of that final. The effect on the people of Denmark was truly overwhelming. There were cheers, there were tears, there were people singing and dancing in the middle of streets. I heard people chanting, "Deutschland Deutschland alles ist vorbei", which at the time I didn't understand. I didn't understand it because it was German, not Danish and meant, "Germany Germany everything is finished." The euphoria was uncontainable as total strangers embraced and celebrated as one.

This might go some way to explain how it was that I met two very well-to-do girls who were themselves celebrating the prodigious victory. The spa at the golf resort was just off to the side of the indoor swimming pool and was open all hours. Each of the guests at the resort had keys to access the pool complex and given that it was rather secluded, there was no curfew imposed. I never did find out how old Anne and Tine were, but by their looks, conduct and wit, I guessed they must have been about 19 or 20. It was their idea to take a spa and I couldn't decline their invitation, particularly as Nicole had left. I returned to our cabin, as did they to theirs, to get changed into appropriate clothing for the spa. On my return, the girls were already in the spa sipping champagne from plastic cups. They had not been able to find champagne glasses, or any glasses for that matter, but we were not complaining. I slid into the warm bubbling waters and took a cup of champagne. After having just watched Denmark win the European Championships, during which I had consumed a number of

Grøn Tuborg beers, the heat of the spa and the cold of the champagne quickly had an effect. When I noticed we had all finished our first cup of champagne, I turned and reached for the bottle. When I turned back around, the girls had removed their bikini tops and were sitting there quite comfortably exposed before me. This was extraordinarily new territory for me – not because the girls were topless, I had seen that before – but because of the romantic connotations in those surroundings and that there were two of them. It was fairly clear that the circumstances had taken me somewhat by surprise, but nonetheless Anne leant over and tentatively kissed me on the neck. Tine repositioned herself from beside Anne to the other side of me and duplicated Anne's actions in kissing me on the neck. The following two hours were most enjoyable, as was the second bottle of champagne. Much to my dismay, however, I learned that they were leaving the resort the next day. More disappointing still, was that they lived just minutes outside of Copenhagen, the Danish capital. It was entirely likely I would not see them again.

Many sore heads were evident around the country the next day, mine included. I was so very grateful for the morning banquet of cereal, eggs, toast and juice, but had to pass on the traditional Schnapps. I spent almost two hours after breakfast listening to music, reading the daily papers that were comprehensively dominated by the epic win the night before and simply relaxing. I then went to the pool, swam for about an hour, and returned to the house for a rare afternoon nap.

As I was resting, I reflected again on the enormity of the win and how, for Denmark, it seemed the anthem of that year's European Championships rang true – it really was 'more than a game'. My mind then wandered to thoughts of that anthem and the applicability of it to my exchange. It was nearing the halfway mark, and I reflected that my exchange was 'more than a year abroad' and on any reasonably objective view, more than a normal exchange. As I began processing those thoughts, a wave of gratitude and contentment for my incredible reality washed over me and I drifted off to sleep.

On our final day at HimmerLand, I joined Carl and Marie for a very early morning round of golf. It was my first real chance to put my new skills to the test and did so with mixed results. Of course, I was always comfortable in the knowledge that, for me, it was more about spending time with my host parents than it was about playing well. However, it was very much a 'warm up' for Carl who was playing in his final round of the weekend tournament that day. Later that afternoon, we all met at the clubhouse for an early dinner as we still had to drive back that day and would be too tired once home. As I was eating my meal, a hand reached over the table and grabbed a hot potato chip from my plate. The hand belonged to Tommy Troelsen, who had been a highly successful football player in Denmark, including being on the 1960 Danish Olympic team that won the silver medal. He was then one of Denmark's most popular television sports commentators and a good friend of Carl's. He was an avid golfer and had enjoyed many rounds of golf under Carl's hospitality at the Aarhus Golf Club. Tommy joined us for the remainder of lunch, and we enjoyed very light-hearted conversation. At one point, he asked me the question that I had been asked dozens of times on exchange – why did you choose Denmark? The first six or seven times I was asked that question, my answer was simply, "I didn't" and little more explanation was offered. Sensing some disappointment, or at the very least, unanswered curiosity in those people, I decided that a more considered answer was needed. Not a convenient answer about why I chose Denmark – that would not have been truthful, nor fair. I explained that Denmark chose me, or rather a Rotarian in my sponsor club who was married to a Dane and thought that I would be a good fit for exchange in Denmark, did. Importantly, I would always add that I was grateful every day that such a decision had been made for me. So that was the answer I gave Tommy, and he seemed to appreciate the honesty of the response. It was a pleasure meeting him and, while I did not and could not have known at the time, it was not going to be the last occasion on which I would meet with him. Our early dinner itself was delightful as we savoured not only the flavours of fine Danish food and beverage, but simply absorbed the last of the sunshine from that perfect summer's day.

I thoroughly enjoyed my few days at HimmerLand and was grateful for the fact that the family was planning another visit there the very next week. My host family had taken a liking to Matthew over his short visits with us and invited him to join us on that next trip. Matthew was very thankful for the opportunity and readily accepted the kind invitation.

Given it was summer holidays, and the conditions were simply sensational, the golf resort was a hive of activity – even more than the weekend prior. Hundreds of people, from young children to older retirees, were enjoying the many different activities available to them. A new attraction since my last visit, and just off the eighteenth hole near the club house, was a mechanical rodeo bull. It was not a permanent feature but there for a couple of weeks over the summer. The attraction was intended for those golfers completing the course at that hole, but before long, Matthew and I were riding it at will. The operator actually enjoyed us doing so as it attracted more attention being used than simply sitting there. The mechanical bull was operated by a number of controls, each with their own speed settings. Each of the controls managed an action or movement of the bull, such as forward and backward, side to side and spinning clockwise or anti-clockwise. The various functions could all be set to the same level, or varied, so that one movement would be more difficult than another. Initially, the settings were rather timid, but after it became apparent to the operator that we were becoming proficient at riding it, he increased the difficulty. In the end, he had the settings reflect a similar level of difficulty that would be experienced in a rodeo ring. He was enormously impressed, as was the crowd that had gathered, when I was able to last five seconds. I was told this would be competitive in the real rodeo arena. Matthew, too, had taken up the challenge with considerable success, but on his final ride, the bull threw him, causing a minor injury. As Matthew was thrown, the hindquarter of the bull caught his foot, thrusting his knee into his nose and making it bleed fairly heavily. It didn't take long for the bleeding to stop, though, as there was no serious damage done.

Carl played golf every day, and while Matthew and I couldn't summon the same amount of dedication, we did enjoy a few rounds with both Carl and Marie. Knowing that my only golf experience was that which was gained the weekend prior, I was given an enormous handicap. I did justice to the handicap on the first three holes as I made several air swings and sliced the ball when it was finally hit. I therefore came under some scrutiny when all of a sudden I birdied the par four, fourth hole. I quickly reverted to the form that saw me start the game under a heavy handicap but did manage to par the seventh hole. In the end, with my handicap considered, I came second. On the specially designed putting green just near the club house, I performed surprisingly well. It was a putting course only, with each of the nine holes having its own par for a total course par of 18. Some holes were a par one, while one of the difficult holes was a par three. I completed the course with a card of 19, only one over par. Based on that performance, I would have been a reasonable golfer – that is if the game only involved putting.

There was only one day where Carl was not able to play any golf. Instead, we took a sight-seeing drive to Skagen in the very northernmost part of Denmark, to where Mikkel and his girlfriend Mianne were enjoying a camping holiday. Denmark is an extraordinarily flat country and its landscape is quite constant. Importantly though, travelling either by car or by train in Denmark is a pleasant experience as the countryside is simply so beautiful. On our way northward, we stopped to visit Aalborg, which was the largest city of the north and the fourth largest city in Denmark. Despite being the largest city in the north, it had a population of less than 150,000 people. It was distinctly historic, dating back more than a thousand years. We didn't have a lot of time in Aalborg but enough to get a feel for the city. We walked along Jomfru Ane Gade, which was one of the most popular and famous streets in Aalborg, if not in all of Denmark. The name Jomfru Ane Gade translates to Virgin Anne's Street, and it was lined with dozens of cafes and bars. By day, the street was reasonably quiet, but I was told that at night and especially on the weekends, it was a 'take-no-prisoners party street'. The presence of a large university in Aalborg helped ensure there were always good crowds of young people frequenting the street. Given Denmark's unique geographical position in Scandinavia, a natural phenomenon could be observed when standing on the very northernmost point of the landmass. At Skagen, the North Sea and the Baltic Sea met in a display of waves and whitewash like two positive forces each trying to repel the other. Interestingly, at that point, it was possible to walk from east to west of Denmark in a matter of seconds given that east and west met at that beachside pinnacle of the north. We ate a delightful lunch with Mikkel and Mianne at their campsite and returned to HimmerLand late that afternoon.

As it turned out, my first host brother and his girlfriend and some of their friends were also camping at small beachside village not far from HimmerLand. Erik had mentioned his camping trip to me many weeks before, and we had agreed that if circumstances permitted, I might spend a night with them. There was a bus route directly from HimmerLand to Løkken, which Matthew and I took early the following day. Løkken was a small town, originally not much more than a little fishing village. In the summer months, it had become a favourite destination for holidaymakers and just to the north of the town was a dedicated camping site right on the beach. The weather was to die for, and we all enjoyed beach games and swimming in the ocean – which for Matthew and me was the first time since Italy. The water was fresh, but not uncomfortably cold. Most of the Danish girls on the beach were without their tops as they made the most of the delightful conditions. I had experienced that Danish beach culture back in Aarhus, but it was the first time that Matthew experienced a Danish beach in summer. That night we joined what appeared to be hundreds of other partygoers at the tavern. Our group was essentially the same group of friends I had learned many a drinking game from when I lived with Bendt and Clara. I was therefore on notice of what was to come, although for Matthew it was all new ground. The alcohol at the tavern was highly priced, even for Danish standards. As a result, we decided to only spend a few hours there making the most of the music and atmosphere. After returning to our campsite, we played further drinking games into the early hours of the morning. We had a fantastic night and chose not to crowd Erik and Maja's tent but rather sleep under the Danish sky. Had I not been so tired, and not fallen asleep as quickly as I did, I would have been very content to just lay there and marvel at the millions of stars shining brightly above. The night air proved to be a most miraculous tonic as both Matthew and I woke without showing any signs of our excess the night before. Our heads were clear as was the Danish sky yet again. We had time enough that morning to take in a couple of games of beach tennis and a refreshing swim. At lunchtime though, we had a bus to catch and we bid a reluctant farewell to Erik, Maja and all our friends.

Back at HimmerLand, Matthew and I continued to enjoy the fantastic Danish weather and to improve our golf games. Due to the fact I was the worst player among us, I had the greatest potential for improvement. Proudly, my game did improve and rather significantly so. In one game, I came second only to Carl and that would have been so regardless of my heavy handicap. HimmerLand was a beautiful place to visit and was ever so relaxing. I was able to do as much or as little as I pleased and having that option was delightful.

My exposure to the game of golf didn't end with our return from HimmerLand. It continued to indirectly be a source for several exciting experiences on exchange. In August, Carl invited me to the Aarhus Golf Club to meet with a number of English sailors from a visiting NATO fleet. While I didn't play any golf with them, I made a more than capable caddy as I raced around in a golf buggy with refreshments. I then had plenty of time to get to know them better over a lovely lunch hosted by the golf club. I must have made a reasonable impression because the Captain of the English war ship, the Andromeda, invited me back to the ship for a private tour. Carl and Marie approved, so I got ready and made my way down to the Aarhus Harbour. The various NATO ships were docked side by side, three deep from the docks. The Andromeda was the furthermost from the dock and I therefore had to board an American ship and a German ship in order to access the English one. Much to my delight, the Captain had already notified the officers on board the other ships and they, too, gave me short tours of their respective ships. Once on board the Andromeda, I again met with the Captain and the Strategic Command Officer, who happened to be an Australian. His name was John and he was on a two-year Naval exchange aboard that ship. He was authorised to take me on an unrestricted tour of the ship and, in doing so, showed me everything on board – including the bridge and various missiles. We returned to the great hall aboard the ship and enjoyed a most delightful afternoon tea with many other sailors. I knew that the experience would linger long in my memory. My experience with the sailors was a perfect example of being open to opportunity and how it was often disguised in places one would not usually expect. Golf wasn't a particular interest of mine, but I was particularly interested in being a part of my host family. Because the game was a big part of my host parents' interests, that meant learning a little about the game and being involved with it when I could. In turn, being involved saw me receive an invitation and gain an experience that no other exchange student received. It was just one of the many fortuitous experiences unique only to my exchange.

Toward the end of my stay with Carl and Marie, I was invited to Emma's 18th birthday at her home in Vejle in the south of Denmark. Naturally, not one to shy from a party, I accepted. Matthew and I travelled together by train from Aarhus, which arrived about two hours prior to the party commencing. Our early arrival was lucky, because finding public transport from the station to Emma's house was almost impossible. We decided the walk wouldn't take very long and made our way on foot. It was great to again get together with other exchange students and reflect on our adventures. Reflection, however, was not the only item on the agenda and we all participated in the evening's many activities. There were a few who perhaps enjoyed themselves a bit too much. Giselle, for one, had a little too much to drink and found comfort for her ills in my arms. The time we shared was soon interrupted by her being physically sick and I spent much of the remainder of the night helping Giselle. Those of us who managed to sleep for an hour or two were in the lucky minority. Our luck stemmed not so much from actually getting sleep but from waking to the sight of the others nearing the end of cleaning the house. That in itself was a huge task. The words written in my diary the next night summarised it best: *There were beers, wine bottles, foods of all flavours, lampshades at angles from being bumped and bodies curled up everywhere.* It was a party of such magnitude that we all talked about it long after we returned home.

Carl and Marie had previously arranged to meet me at Billund, a town only a short train trip from Vejle. It was at Billund that I was able to experience, together with Carl, Marie, Johanna and her friend Camilla, the wonder of Legoland. Lego is perhaps one of the country's most renowned exports with children the world over enjoying the unique building blocks from Denmark. While in Latin, Lego means 'I assemble' or 'I put together', the origin of the name was actually the combination of the Danish words 'leg godt', meaning play well. The tourist park opened in June 1968 although the business had been established over 30 years prior. It was a very popular tourist destination and attracted thousands of visitors each day. There were rides and shows, however the real attraction was the many models made of Lego. The models ranged from Danish icons such as Hans Christian Andersen and the Port of Copenhagen, to American wonders like the Statue of Liberty and Mount Rushmore. All told, there were well over 34 million Lego bricks used in construction of the models displayed. Despite having had far too many beers and far too little sleep the night before, I was able to thoroughly enjoy the day at Legoland with my host family.

Given that I was more than halfway through my exchange while living with Carl and Marie, I had many friends and lots of engagements. When I wasn't away on holidays or class excursions, I was often in neighbouring towns visiting Matthew or Michael. These regular absences didn't take from my time with Carl and Marie but added to it. My heart was open from day one on Teglbakken and by the time I had to bid my second host family farewell, it was full of love and appreciation for them. Just as my heart was open from day one, so too their hearts, along with their home. Not surprisingly, it was once again hard to say goodbye and move to my final Danish home.

7

The England Experience

The day before we were to leave for England, Matthew came to stay with me at Carl and Marie's home. I met Matthew at the train station in the city, and together we caught the number 6 bus out to Højberg. The buses in Aarhus had an automated ticketing system where it was up to each passenger to purchase their ticket from a machine located at the rear of the bus. To an unfamiliar traveller, the temptation to evade the fare may be great – even unconscious – given a lack of knowledge of the system. However, it was the potential fine that was great, given out relentlessly by inspectors who boarded the buses without warning and at random stops. Ordinarily, I had a bus pass purchased for me by my Rotary Club, but because it was the school summer holidays, the bus pass had expired and I wasn't due for the next one until I returned to school. Matthew and I boarded the bus at the Aarhus train station to go to my home, and by the next stop, only 300 or 400 metres away, had not purchased our tickets. That wasn't due a to an intention to evade a fare, but because we had Matthew's suitcase open on the floor looking for his wallet. Inspectors boarded at that next stop and refused to show any understanding of our position and fined us heavily for not having purchased tickets. This was extremely disappointing and significantly reduced what little money we had saved for our trip to England.

The next day we were on the number 6 bus again - tickets purchased immediately on boarding this time - returning to the city to catch the airport bus. We were both excited about our impending flight, the first since we had landed in Odense some five months earlier. The flight, again with Scandinavian Airlines System, was over before we knew it. It was an international flight, yet in comparison to the long-haul flights we had taken to get to Denmark, the flight to the United Kingdom was quick. It seemed as though we took off, ate the sandwiches and finished the drinks provided, then commenced the descent for landing. In reality it was a little longer than that – just on two hours. But travelling together ensured that Matthew and I had good conversation and humorous distraction from the flying time.

Heathrow Airport was an adventure more akin to scenes from an action movie. Our first point of call, after clearing customs, was a money exchange where we converted Danish Krone to British Pounds. As Matthew and I made our way through the airport terminal toward the exits, I couldn't remember picking up my passport at the cash exchange. Matthew headed back there, while I rummaged through my backpack. I had not left it behind as feared and turned to chase Matthew. I had taken little more than five or six steps when airport security surrounded our suitcases left only a few metres behind me. It took some explaining but security was quick to believe what had happened. They explained that we should be more careful and not leave cases unattended – even for the briefest of moments – as they were very watchful for terrorist activity all the time. We then found a public telephone and tried to ring Matthew's family friends. The number Matthew had was not correct and directory assistance could not be of any help as their actual number was silent. Matthew was not even certain that the address he had was entirely accurate. We took our chances and boarded the subway bound for the suburb of Romford in Essex. That went off without a hitch and we were left standing at the Romford station, hoping a taxi driver could make sense of the address we were trying to find.

Fate is truly an amazing phenomenon. We approached an old black cab driven by an elderly lady wearing little white gloves and a woven bonnet atop her ash-grey hair. It was so cliché and could have easily been from a movie scene, but it was our reality as we tried to find our way. We tentatively asked whether she knew of the address in Romford we were looking for and she said she did. During the drive to the outer regions of Romford, our adorable old driver was full of conversation and interest in our travels. Conversation turned to who we were visiting in Romford and Matthew informed her that his family's friends were named Ted and Gina. She asked if Ted was a former taxi driver in London, to which Matthew answered in the affirmative. An enormous smile pushed aside the wrinkles that the passing of time had imposed upon her face and our driver said, "Oh, old Teddles, I know 'im." When we arrived in Ted and Gina's driveway, Ted was tending to the garden. Our driver declined Ted's invitation for tea and also our payment of the fare. She was truly a fascinating woman with many stories to share.

The next day was wet, cold and miserable. We had planned to visit London but chose instead to spend the day indoors with Ted and Gina. I very much enjoyed the opportunity to do so as we were to spend the next nine days in their home. Ted was a tall thin man with a seemingly permanent smile on his face. Gina was a caring lady, who almost immediately took to us like her own children. We were given a key to their home and assured that we could come and go as we pleased. Their home was comfortable with a chocolate-brown roof and a white cement rendered exterior. The Tudor styled windows and chimney perfectly complemented the structure. Ted had a great knowledge of the people and places of interest, given that for 20 years he had driven cabs throughout Romford and London. This knowledge allowed him to devise a most interesting and busy itinerary for Matthew and me for the remaining eight days.

Day three as tourists saw us visit the city of London. We boarded a traditional red double decker bus to take in a 'see the sights' guided tour. This tour was suggested by Ted as it offered a good familiarisation with the city and the sites of interest. We were then able to visit those places at our own pace. On the tour, we drove down a street in which one of the shop windows was dressed in images of Queensland and, in particular, of the Gold Coast. The banner across the shop facade read 'Queensland House' and naturally, I felt a warm sense of pride. We were keen to take in our first Hard Rock Cafe experience and made our way there for lunch. Much to our disappointment, the previous day had seen Arnold Schwarzenegger and Slyvester Stallone visit the famous cafe. We may well have visited the cafe the day before had the weather not been so poor – but it wasn't meant to be. We purchased a couple of small thank you gifts for Ted and Gina and returned home mid-way through the afternoon.

We packed a lot into day four of our city sight-seeing schedule. Although the Queen no longer played any active role in Australia's affairs and was only our monarch by historical association, it was with a degree of respect for our history, that Matthew and I visited Buckingham Palace. The lavishness of the Palace and imposing figures of the guards mounted on horseback could not be ignored. Again, with the benefit of local knowledge, we arrived early and secured a good vantage point for the changing of the guard. It was impressive, not only for the pomp and ceremony of the event, but for the richness of the tradition that dated back hundreds of years. It was intriguing to see that the changing of the guard appealed to such a wide gamut of people, as I observed both young and old enjoy the occasion. We made our way to Big Ben and then to Trafalgar Square, where we stopped for a bite to eat. Most of what was left of the day was spent admiring the Tower of London and its exhibits. The dungeon, the jewel house, the very fact we were there was just overwhelming. The hundreds of years of history was simply awe inspiring and I knew that every intricate detail would long remain in my memory. We had plenty of time remaining on our holiday in England, so we were not too concerned to see everything all at once. There were only a few sights of interest to Matthew and me that remained to be seen, including Madame Tussauds Wax Museum and St. Paul's Cathedral.

Two days of London in a row were enough, so day five was spent locally in Romford. We went to an entertainment centre where Matthew and I played a laser combat game and met a couple of girls who asked us to the movies later that night. Naturally, the prospect of getting to know some locals could only broaden our perspectives and experiences and we gladly accepted the invitation. We met Natalie and Tracey at the Romford train station as arranged and went with them to the cinema. Strangely, they appeared to be complete opposites. Natalie was only slightly shorter than me, had very long black hair and fair porcelain-like skin. She wore an enormous smile which showed off pure white and perfectly straight teeth. Natalie demonstrated an abundant personality and seemed to do most of the talking for both of them. Tracey on the other hand, was considerably shorter than Natalie, had very short blonde hair and a slightly blemished complexion. She appeared sweet enough, but it was hard to really tell, given that she didn't say a lot. The girls asked us to join them at a club afterwards, but we had told Ted and Gina that we would return straight from the cinema, which we felt compelled to do. We did of course accept their telephone numbers and agreed to call them later in our stay.

Ted and Gina suggested that we might like to visit Cambridge University and offered to drive us out to the famous campus. We gratefully accepted their kind offer and spent a terrific day with them sightseeing. As we drove through the English countryside, Gina commented that we were seeing 'the real England'. It certainly was very beautiful countryside and a most pleasant drive. A highlight of the day was to wander around the Great Court of Trinity College made famous by the story behind the movie *Chariots of Fire*. Countless numbers of people have attempted to run around the historic Court in the forty-three seconds that it took for the bells of the College clock to strike twelve o'clock. Due to a rather odd tradition, the bells in that clock chimed twice for each hour. As I walked the 341 metres around the Court, I tried to imagine the athleticism that would be required to achieve the feat. The first person to display such athleticism was a student at Cambridge University in 1919.

Harold Abrahams went on to be the 100 metre Olympic Champion in the 1924 Olympics. The thought did cross my mind to sprint the path and time my endeavour, but I wasn't dressed appropriately and knew, in any event, that it wouldn't be close to forty-three seconds. We enjoyed a lovely lunch in a quaint, but typical English pub. It was located down a cobblestoned laneway and sat alongside the Cambridge canals. I sampled a traditional Guinness beer that took almost as long as our lunch to be served, not because of poor service, but because of the pour. It took me longer to finish my beer than it took me to finish my lunch, as I quickly discovered that Guinness was not my favourite drop.

On our return home, we all sat on the rear landing of Ted and Gina's home and simply talked for hours. It occurred to me at the time, that this world of ours was very unique, made that way by people of diverse and interesting backgrounds. I made the comment that it was one thing for people to visit places abroad, but it was something altogether different to experience the people of those places. Matthew and I were ever so lucky to be guests of Ted and Gina and to have gained such an insight to the sort of wonderful people they were. It was apparent that Ted and Gina felt similarly about Matthew and me, as Ted brought out his most prized bottle of Glenfiddich which we shared together. We were told that Ted shares his Glenfiddich with very few people indeed. As a whiskey purist, Ted was horrified when I asked for Coke and ice. As a result, I bravely drank it neat. As we sat there though, I couldn't help but reflect once more on how profound the journey of exchange had been, and how it had absolutely continued this way during our short stay in London. The depth of connection made with Ted and Gina in such a short space of time was hard to comprehend.

In no time at all, we were more than half-way through our stay in England and still had some sights to see in London. As it was impossible to predict the future, particularly in respect of the English weather, we decided to make the most of the delightful summer's day that had greeted us that morning and re-visit London. It became obvious to us that the trains of London were as equally unpredictable as the weather. We were en-route to London when our train came to a grinding halt only metres after leaving a station platform. As guards and sniffer dogs boarded the train, we were all directed to climb out and make our way back along the tracks to the safety of the station. The almost routine way in which the other passengers went about executing these directions made us think that perhaps this was not an isolated event and that there was nothing to actually be worried about. Nevertheless, we found it terribly exciting. We never did discover why we were forced to stop and alight that train, although the presence of sniffer dogs suggests it wasn't general maintenance. We were made aware that the line would probably be closed for at least an hour, maybe longer. We decided to catch a train in the other direction and return to Romford.

Once home, Gina suggested that we visit the local markets, which we thoroughly enjoyed. Given that we had some time left that day, we telephoned Natalie and Tracey. Natalie seemed excited to hear from us again and suggested we join them at a big wrestling event being held that night in Romford. 'Big Daddy' was the popular local wrestler and together with the enormous 300+ kilogram wrestler called 'Giant Haystacks', drew a large crowd to the entertainment centre. We didn't hear the official numbers in attendance, but I guessed there would have been about three to five thousand people. Wrestling was not really a sport that interested me, but being there that night was most entertaining. As we exited the venue though, we encountered eight or ten young teenagers. They looked like they were only about thirteen or fourteen years old, but despite their apparent youth, came up to Matthew and me and rather audaciously started fighting us. I thought they were just playing, until one of them 'coat-hangered' me in the mouth with his forearm. The combination of pain and the taste of blood in my mouth signalled it was necessary to defend myself. When the next child assailant came at me, I picked him up and threw him onto a chain fence. I turned to see Matthew restraining two more and after thumping one more, they gave up and ran away. Matthew and I were discussing how random the attack was, when Tracey spoke up and said that she recognised one of them as a neighbour, a couple of doors down from where she lived. She thought that perhaps her neighbour had some romantic, albeit naive interest in her and jealously caused him and his friends to start the fight. The cut inside my mouth was only small, as was the bruise on my wrist.

On this occasion, we had told Ted and Gina that we may be late home, particularly if the girls wanted to continuing partying after the wrestling. Indeed, they did and we went to a local nightspot called Legends. It was a great club, with an Australian D.J. in control of the music. We introduced ourselves to him and were treated to free drinks and plenty of attention throughout the night. Natalie and I became very close that evening and although she was an exceptional kisser, I declined her invitation to take it one step further. Her invitation would have involved leaving Matthew at the club and going to her unit in a part of Romford I knew nothing about. I had already stretched the boundaries of my personal safety by stepping into the darkness of a laneway behind the club with her. Going to her place was simply not an option, as difficult as it was to decline.

Given the late hour of our return, Matthew and I woke much later than we had planned. We decided that the day would be too rushed if we tried to visit London. Instead, Ted let me drive his car and we ventured out to a local market. I knew that driving was against the Rotary rules for exchange, but given they drive on the same side of the road as we did in Australia, it didn't seem as risky. Matthew purchased a fine suit, which was very reasonably priced. I was tempted by several items at the market but remained disciplined enough not to buy them. We returned home after renting some videos and simply spent the rest of the day at home. It was not such a waste of an afternoon, considering the weather was not nearly as inviting as it had been that morning.

We were determined not to leave England without once again making the trip into the city to visit the remaining places of interest to Matthew and me. Luckily the weather was kind the next day, as was the hassle-free train ride to the city. We arrived in London quite early and wasted no time in getting to Madame Tussauds on Baker Street. It was unrealistic to believe that wax figures could look so realistic, yet therein was the irony as we were juxtaposed in a world surrounded by famous people - although they were made of wax. There were the icons known the world over, such as Superman and the Royal Family, but also Australian characters such as Crocodile Dundee and Kylie Minogue. Even Denmark got a showing with her famous storytelling son, Hans Christian Anderson also featured. As planned, we also took in the famous St Paul's Cathedral, a prominent landmark in London. Not only prominent for its magnificent architecture and imposing presence, the Cathedral was equally prominent for the many notable services held there. Famously, the eyes of the world were on the Cathedral when Prince Charles and Lady Diana were married in 1981. Although not attracting the world's media in the same way, the funeral of Sir Winston Churchill in 1965 was also held at that Cathedral as part of a State Service. We made an impromptu visit to Greenwich, the Royal Observatory and the home of Greenwich Mean Time. The observatory and other landmarks of Greenwich would go on to be added to the UNESCO list of protected places. I was rather pleased that Matthew and I had decided to visit Greenwich, especially since it hadn't been a priority. We enjoyed ourselves greatly as the day was entirely unhurried, which allowed us to simply get a feel for the city of our colonial forefathers.

Our return flight to Denmark wasn't scheduled until 2:00pm but having experienced first-hand the unpredictability of the London trains, we decided to leave quite early. Knowing how hard it was to say goodbye to my host family in Odense, and Bendt and Clara in Aarhus, it came as no surprise that it was similarly difficult to farewell Ted and Gina. While our time with them was significantly less than with our host families, we had nonetheless been shown hospitality and kindness of the highest order. They were very special people, and I just knew I would miss them in the future. As with all the incredible people I met on exchange, hope was always held that a future meeting would happen one day.

Heathrow Airport was exactly as it was when we arrived those ten days earlier - big and busy. As the main gateway to England by air, it was hardly surprising that thousands of people passed through the famous airport daily. We wasted no time checking in our luggage and obtaining our boarding passes. It was not that we were running at all late, simply that we wanted to be able to relax and take our time. We boarded our plane following the second boarding call and settled in for the flight home. Once in the air, Matthew and I decided to indulge ourselves and shared a small bottle of red wine with our gourmet sandwiches. It was not long after we opened the bottle of red wine that the adventure started. There were some small bumps and rumblings as the plane entered mild turbulence, but no one seemed at all perturbed. Our senses were heightened somewhat because Matthew and I were sitting in seats that overlooked one of the wings of the plane. Even the mild turbulence appeared to result in the wing flapping as would a small bird in flight. Still, this was of no concern to us. We were concerned though, when the pilot asked that all trays be collected and fold-away tables be returned to the upright position as the turbulence was expected to worsen. It was not as though the weather was that ominous, but the atmosphere was obviously quite unstable. Without warning, the plane felt as though it dropped many metres, although in reality it was probably no more than a small dip. It did, however, make a most thunderous thud before again levelling out. That drop had at least put us on notice of what was to come and it was then that many of the passengers started to openly display their fear. Matthew and I remained calm, probably dismissing our concerns with a youthful sense of adventure. Either that or neither of us wanted to admit being frightened to the other. Before long, the wing that was so clearly visible to us was bouncing around more akin to the wings of a spooked sparrow and the plane was banking violently to the left and right. Luckily, Matthew and I only had to maintain our composure for a few minutes; suddenly, the plane again levelled out and the cabin was still. The entire turbulent time was probably no more than five or six minutes, but for many it seemed so much longer. Without further incident, we landed in our new homeland, disembarked and caught the airport bus back into the city.

Upon our return to Carl and Marie's, we were welcomed with the aromas of Marie's wonderful cooking. We had confirmed prior to leaving Heathrow, that we expected to be home on time. Matthew was staying with us that evening, and was a welcomed dinner guest. Conversation centred on our holiday, the great experiences we had enjoyed and of course the flight back to Aarhus. That night, as had become my custom, I penned the adventures of that day in my diary and closed the pages of yet another chapter in my ever-increasing special exchange year.

8

Getting Together

Twice each year in Denmark, all exchange students are invited to get together as one great group. Rarely do any students miss these events. Given there is always sufficient notice, most ensure their calendars are clear on the dates upon which they fall.

The first 'get-together' for 1992 was held from Friday, 13 March to Sunday, 15 March in a small Danish town called Ikast. It was unquestionably one of the most memorable experiences of exchange yet at the same time a true test of endurance.

I woke at about 7:00am on Friday and went to language school in the city. That was the only school I went to that day. My absence from the gymnasium was excused by the fact that the get-together was an approved Rotary event. The school principal had made it clear that the school would be very flexible in terms of my attendance. Of course, there was an expectation that I attended while in Aarhus. That was an expectation shared by Rotary, both in Denmark and at home in Australia and was a requirement of my student visa. Quite apart from the expectation of others, it was my own expectation to attend as much as possible, because I was fortunate to have such tremendous classmates. This get together, though, was one of the many acceptable reasons for me not to attend school. I had my bags for Ikast with me at language school, because I didn't have time to go home before catching the train to Ikast.

As an exchange student, the attention of strangers was not uncommon. However, while standing on the platform of the Aarhus train station waiting for my train, I attracted the type of attention I would rather have avoided. Throughout the more populated cities of Denmark were impoverished vagabonds. They would collect all manner of paraphernalia and affix it to their tattered coats and jackets in much the same way as exchange students would affix badges, pins and patches to their exchange jackets. As I came to learn, they, in their own way, swap items from their jackets as and when they may meet. More importantly, they held firm the belief that the wearing of collectables on clothing was an act exclusive to their demographic. Therefore, proudly wearing what had already become a very decorated Rotary exchange jacket proved somewhat offensive to one particular itinerant. With only a limited command of Danish, understanding the mumblings of an old and dirty vagabond was virtually impossible. Fortuitously for me, an American exchange student was catching the same train headed for the same gathering in Ikast. Melissa had been on exchange for some nine months and was far more proficient in the language than me. As a result, she was able to ease the tension slightly and provide an explanation to station staff. It was certainly not the type of attention my jacket normally attracted.

Friday evening was almost exclusively spent partying. No time was wasted in catching up with those friends met at language camp and in meeting dozens of new friends. Again, the commonality of what we were all doing facilitated mutual understanding and formed an irresistible basis for new friendships to be made and existing friendships to be strengthened. At about 5:00am, I decided that I needed some sleep, knowing that at that time it would only be short. It was indeed short – one hour – before I was woken by the others waking up from their longer and more restful sleep.

As much as it predominated proceedings, the weekend wasn't entirely about partying. The Rotarians from the Rotary Club of Ikast had kindly arranged for a tour of the town, which included a visit to Town Hall. We were told that the local government area of Ikast had a population of around 15,000 inhabitants and that its major industries were agriculture and textiles. Having achieved only one hour of sleep the night before, interest in the tour was hard to sustain. When the lecture about Ikast turned to a discussion about its local government, most of what was said was largely missed - not because we were being rude but simply from a lack of ability to comprehend.

We were all staying in a local school for the weekend with various classrooms converted to make-shift dormitories. In reality, the conversion was little more than moving all the tables and chairs into the centre of the rooms and laying down small rubber mats on the floor to sleep on. But given that most students enjoyed very little sleep anyway, the accommodation was adequate.

When it began to snow outside, six of us decided to enjoy ourselves in it and exercise our creative sides at the same time. Michael, Allan and I were joined by three girls from the United Sates – Carrie from Albuquerque, Megan from Oregon and Simone from Michigan – out in the snow. We actually took a few chairs from one of the classrooms and placed them in the snow – perfect props for photo taking. Our first series of photos involved the girls sitting in the chairs with the boys standing behind them and then the roles were reversed. It was after those photographs were taken when the fun began. As Michael, Allan and I sat there, the girls decided to grab the back of the chairs and pull us backwards, causing us to fall onto the ground. Another student who was kindly taking our photos said that she had not taken the photograph with all six cameras, so we were seated again. However, just as she was about to take photographs again, the girls this time pushed our chairs forward and we again fell into the snow. We chased the girls and tackled them into the snow before spending the next half an hour or so running around in a snowball throwing war. Our seated photographs were taken while Michael, Allan and I were proudly wearing our Rotary jackets, which by that stage were very well decorated. Luckily, we had the good presence of mind to remove those as we ran and rolled around outside.

Saturday evening was indescribable. We danced, sang, ate, drank and thoroughly enjoyed each other's company. For the first time in many months, I again found myself dancing the Jive, the Cha Cha and even an exhibition Waltz, but this time with a number of different partners. As is traditional at almost any exchange student gathering, we all formed small groups and hurriedly prepared skits to perform in the evening concert. It was truly comforting to perform to an audience comprised entirely of friends. This was especially so for those who, like me, were not otherwise comfortable performing to anyone. The fits of laughter were not at us, but with us, as we all enjoyed the lighter side of life. There were, of course, some students who were natural performers and we enjoyed a number of very good performances by musicians, singers and even a poet.

A sore and sorry handful of us were instrumental in dragging the party from Saturday evening into the early hours of Sunday morning. That said, I was able to enjoy four times the amount of sleep I had had the night before – a comparatively welcomed four hours. Those precious hours were spent in Leanne's sleeping bag. We had met that day and become very friendly throughout the evening, sharing much more than the occasional dance and suggestive glance. It was not surprising that we ultimately shared the same sleeping quarters. It was an easy decision to spend what was left of the night with Leanne but not nearly as easy to actually make it happen. There were Rotarians present at the school virtually the whole time we were there, especially so as the hour grew late and students were going to bed. The boys' rooms were at the opposite end of a long corridor from the girls' rooms and Rotarians sat in that corridor to prevent students getting 'lost' in the wrong rooms. I had to devise another way to get to Leanne. It was bitterly cold; a thin layer of snow blanketed the ground outside and a little more was falling. Wearing nothing but my boxer shorts, I climbed out of the window and ran through the snow to Leanne's room. There was only a moment's commotion as I knocked on the closed window to the girls' room. Most of the girls had long before fallen asleep, but I had assured Leanne that I would find a way and she quietly opened the window and allowed me in. Whether or not it had been our intention to share her sleeping bag was irrelevant. It was, by that stage, a necessity, because I was frightfully cold. I needed the warmth of Leanne, and her sleeping bag, to bring the shivers and the chattering of my teeth under control. The warmth quickly returned to my being, and Leanne and I enjoyed each other's company and some well needed sleep. There were two or three other girls still awake but despite their disapproving glances, they didn't complain. Despite retiring so late, I was able to rise early, sneak back to my room through the snow and beat the rush to the showers. There were only a handful of showers available for some 100 students, so it was essential to get in early to ensure the continuous supply of hot water.

Sunday drew to a close rather rapidly and forgivingly. I had, from waking at 7:00am on Friday morning only managed five hours of sleep come breakfast time Sunday. Breakfast was the only event shared by the group that day before farewells were said. It remained for me to face the long train ride back to Aarhus. I used that time penning letters to those at home and in part, reflecting upon the Ikast weekend. Contrary to what might be expected of such a tired author, the letter captured the moment:

> That weekend was exactly what being an exchange student is all about! The comradeship and bonding experienced was so powerful...some parts of the weekend gave way to emotional periods, where those who were together for the last time on their exchange gave way to tears and sadness. However, in the true spirit of exchange, the youthful spirit in everyone could not be subdued...experience mixed

> with inexperience to culminate in a weekend beyond useful description.

The reference in my letter to 'experience mixed with inexperience' was based on the fact that approximately half of the students at the 'get-together' had been on exchange for about nine months. Students from countries in the Northern Hemisphere would embark on their exchange in their summer – June of one year, until June in the following year. Students from the Southern Hemisphere would exchange in their summer – January of one year to January of the next year. Those students from the Northern Hemisphere countries were colloquially known as the 'Summer Group', while those of us from the Southern Hemisphere were referred to as the 'Winter Group', both based upon the season in which we arrived in Denmark. This perpetual mix of 'old' and 'new' students ensured the sharing of information, experiences and advice. It also ensured any legendary tales of adventure or woe would be passed from one cohort of exchange students to the next. So, as much as the weekend 'get-togethers' were about fun and friendship, there was an immutable learning aspect to them.

It would be some seven months before we would be fortunate enough to repeat the adventure and to get to share our experience and knowledge with the 'new' Summer Group. It wasn't until Friday, 23 October 1992 that we again met in that fashion. But meet we did, only this time I was among the experienced group. There were dozens of exchange students who had, as I had done in March, only recently arrived in Denmark. It was a prodigious experience sharing knowledge and taking on a mentor role for those needing it. Few experts are entitled to that designation with only ten months experience, but amazingly, it seemed an appropriate description for us. Perhaps it was consistent with every other aspect of exchange. Deep and meaningful connections are made more intensely and quickly than there are in 'non-exchange' settings. Incredibly close relationships with host families and friends are forged in a fraction of the time it would otherwise take. All of that, of course, is predicated on the ability of the student to open their hearts and minds quickly, trust completely and adapt entirely to their new life. This knowledge gained from unique experience was too valuable not to share. I saw it as an obligation to demonstrate all that was special about exchange. A responsibility to guide and to give tips and pointers, and important insights into how I had come to have an extraordinary time up to that point of my exchange.

The weekend, while vastly different in perspective, was identical in its lead-up and execution. My language tuition at the language course had finished, but I had become even closer to my class at Marselisborg Gymnasium. I wanted to attend, if only to wish them a good weekend. After that, Matthew and Michael met me in the city mid-morning and, to pass the time, we played a few games of pool at Lion's – a bar that had become very much a regular venue for me. Unlike the Ikast weekend, we had to travel by ferry and train to reach our Holbæk destination. Although only about 130 kilometres away, the trip actually took over three hours to complete because it involved both a ferry journey and a train ride. The ferry was the longest leg of the journey but passed rather quickly because there were many students onboard. Some of the behaviour on the train ride bordered on stupidity but was nonetheless enjoyable. It transpired that, remarkably, we managed to fit 17 of us into a cabin with a seating capacity of six. The windows were the type that allowed foolish students to hang out of them and take the wind in their faces. Not the smartest thing to do when whizzing by power poles every few hundred metres. In much the same way as our train cabin had been cramped, we squeezed three or four additional bodies into one of the cars that was available to shuttle us from the train station to the school at which the weekend was being held.

There was no visit to the municipal headquarters for Holbæk, rather two city officials visited us at our get-together location. They explained that Holbæk was a commercial and industrial centre for the surrounding areas and was a major hub for various bus routes. Given its position on the banks of the beautiful Holbæk Fjord, the city also boasted an active commercial seaport. We were told that the origins of the city dated back to 1199 at which time it was called Holbækgaard. At that time, it was essentially just a large farm owned by a nobleman, around which the city eventually developed.

Unlike the first evening at the Ikast weekend, I got absolutely no sleep Friday night. It was an extraordinary night of revelling in friendship that culminated in the birth of a new superhero. In an effort to remain awake and keep things interesting, 'Australia Man' was discovered. It was not a particularly creative costume, but in the early hours of Saturday morning, I tied a large Australian Flag around my neck and proudly ran about with it flowing behind me as a cape. It came as quite a shock the next morning when people were again calling for an appearance by 'Australia Man'. So, with the faithful in tow, 'Australia Man' made his way into town. No lives were saved, nor disasters averted, but much fun was had by not only the exchange students but many locals as well. Of course, I happened to enjoy the adventure that later became the stuff of legend.

We returned to the school campus at which the get-together was being held. Again, the Saturday evening was the traditional night for Rotarians to visit and for ad-hoc entertainment to be staged by the students. In every exchange group, there are always a number of talented students who simply amaze their peers. One of the new Canadian students played the guitar and harmonica simultaneously and managed to also sing a song that he had written. He then sang *Country Roads* by John Denver. It was one of the most moving live performances I had ever encountered. Perhaps it was his talent, perhaps the circumstances, perhaps a combination of both of those things – but whatever the reason, there was hardly a dry eye in the room. When he so melodically sang the words, *country roads, take me home, to the place, I belong...* I looked around the room to see my friends in mixed states of emotion. I wondered whether it was the fact that for some, it may have brought to mind memories of home, or like me, it highlighted a real paradox in belief. I felt very much at home being in Denmark but was forced to recognise that home was, in fact, Australia. Those thoughts though were fleeting, as we quite automatically linked arms and started singing along. For those few minutes of our existence, there was nothing else on the planet. We were not in West Virginia, not in Denmark, not in Australia or anywhere. We were just in a state of being – a state of being exchange students and very much together in that feeling. Not surprisingly, his standing ovation lasted almost as long as the song.

Exchange students would always sing two other songs at the end of the get-together concerts. The first was creatively titled *Exchangee Song* or some variation of that theme. Its origins were unknown – certainly to me – but it was no doubt one of the many legacies handed down from one generation of exchange students to the next. It had really evolved over that time, with the lyrics having been passed from one group to another over many years. Verses were added, removed or amended from time to time, but the core theme remained. Some suggested it was more a poem than a song and should therefore be recited, not sung. I figured it depended more on the 'performers' of the day than on form. Ultimately, I only ever heard it sung. While for the rare rogue or two, the song was something of a mantra to live by, most of us knew that the song was very much a parody of our existence.

I had seen several different versions of the same song. I did see a version circulated through another exchange organisation and hoped those lyrics would never find their way into 'our' song. Their version, or at least parts of it, quite simply crossed the line from light-hearted parody to an obscene and tasteless insult on the exchange experience. Given that the *Exchangee Song* was regularly performed at exchange student gatherings, heard by Rotarians, parents and others apart from the students, it was important not to go too far. Some of the verses in 'our' song came close to the line but didn't cross it in the context of the song.

Our group settled on a song composed with thirteen stanzas. That really represented numerically, a stanza for each amazing month of exchange, plus an extra one – the last – to really give balance to the song. A serious end to an otherwise silly song.

Exchangees, exchangees a long way from home
We're totally disorganised, so leave us alone
We drink when we're thirsty, we drink when we're dry
We drink till we're drunk and then we get h...

Aye, aye, aye-aye
We are exchangees, exchangees
We live it up, we live it up, we live it up we do
So pass another Tuborg

We're highly obnoxious, we're crazy and queer
We really get up to some Tuborg beer
No drinking, no driving, no dating, no grass
The Rotary rules are a pain in the a...

Aye, aye, aye-aye
We are exchangees, exchangees
We live it up, we live it up, we live it up we do
So pass another Tuborg

If the ocean was whiskey and I was a duck
I'd swim to the bottom and drink my way up
But the ocean's not whiskey and I'm not a duck
So let's go to Denmark and have a good f...

Aye, aye, aye-aye

We are exchangees, exchangees
We live it up, we live it up, we live it up we do
So pass another Tuborg

Some day we'll be doctors, some day engineers
But right at this moment we're into our beers
We're learning the language as best as we can
But right at the moment, we don't give a d...

Aye, aye, aye-aye
We are exchangees, exchangees
We live it up, we live it up, we live it up we do
So pass another Tuborg

We go on the tour and we have lots of fun
To all the best places in Europe we come
We spend all our money, but don't give a hoot
Cause Mummy and Daddy will give us more loot...

Aye, aye, aye-aye
We are exchangees, exchangees
We live it up, we live it up, we live it up we do
So pass another Tuborg

Exchangees, exchangees all crammed in a bus
All laughing and loving and burning with lust
We hug and we kiss and we tell dirty jokes
We break all the rules, but don't tell our folks...

Aye, aye, aye-aye
We are exchangees, exchangees
We live it up, we live it up, we live it up we do
So pass another Tuborg

Exchangees, exchangees all stuck in our schools
We try to speak Danish, but all look like fools
The teachers all hate us, we're never in class
But if you don't like it, then just kiss our a...

Aye, aye, aye-aye
We are exchangees, exchangees
We live it up, we live it up, we live it up we do
So pass another Tuborg

Host brothers and sisters we love them a lot
As a matter of fact, it can get pretty hot
We like to give kisses, perhaps even two
But too many kisses, gets us in deep p...

Aye, aye, aye-aye
We are exchangees, exchangees
We live it up, we live it up, we live it up we do
So pass another Tuborg

If the world was much smaller and I was a dove
I'd fly to each country and send them my love
But the world ain't much smaller and I ain't no dove
So let's go to Denmark and have a good...

Aye, aye, aye-aye
We are exchangees, exchangees
We live it up, we live it up, we live it up we do
So pass another Tuborg

We like to eat chocolate, we like to eat cake
We like to eat ice-cream and gain lots of weight

*Our butts may be fat and our thighs may grow
But give us a chance and we'll let it all show...*

*Aye, aye, aye-aye
We are exchangees, exchangees
We live it up, we live it up, we live it up we do
So pass another Tuborg*

*Exchangees like us, we do something wrong
But give us a chance and we'll sing you a song
The song that we sing, we think is a hit
But tell you the truth, it's probably sh...*

*Aye, aye, aye-aye
We are exchangees, exchangees
We live it up, we live it up, we live it up we do
So pass another Tuborg*

*But all this is rubbish, we're loving our stay
The pace is so hectic, we're sober all day
We're virgins, we promise and we'd all like to say
Just how much we appreciate, this wonderful stay...*

*Aye, aye, aye-aye
We are exchangees, exchangees
We live it up, we live it up, we live it up we do
So pass another Tuborg*

*If it wasn't for Rotary, we wouldn't be here
We wouldn't be having such a wonderful year
No drinking, no drugs, no sex to be had
These Rotary rules aren't really that bad.*

The unofficial anthem for exchange was Don McLean's classic song *American Pie*. Again, I had no idea where the tradition came from but really didn't care. Virtually all students would link arms over each other's shoulders and sing together. Sometimes *American Pie* was used to signal the end of the night and, at other times, only the end of the staged concert part of the night. At Holbæk it was the latter. Actually, it couldn't have been anything but the latter, given I was one of several students who didn't, at any stage, end the night.

I noticed that one of the Brazilian students knew the Jive and Cha Cha, so she was squarely in my sights for the party later that night. Angela and I danced until my legs were numb and we became very close friends. Our display, however, brought out more Latin dancers among the group and I had to dig deep into my reserves of energy to dance extensively with another two students from Brazil. Fernanda and Viviane were both trained dancers, but it was Fernanda who really had me working on the floor. She was as good a dancer as she was gorgeous and I certainly drew the envy of many of the other male exchange students during the display of spirited dancing with Fernanda. So many times throughout the night, I smiled cheekily, remembering the words my mother had said some years before to convince me to take up ballroom dancing. Basically, my mother had assured me that knowing how to dance, would at some stage, set me apart from most other young men my age. As most mothers ultimately are, Mum was right.

It was thirsty work and of course, the beer on tap flowed freely. Such was its accessibility that Michael and I were able to drink directly from the Carlsberg tap more than once. The dancing, singing and partying continued unabated until the sun made an appearance Sunday morning. With the sight of the morning sun came the painful realisation that another night had passed without me having any sleep. The exhaustion hit immediately. There was no place to hide as we only had time enough to clean up from the night before and pack our luggage before breakfast.

Matthew, Michael and I had to endure a two hour wait at the ferry terminal in Kalundborg in order to return home. Remaining awake and coherent was perhaps one of the most difficult things I had been called upon to do. The wait was made a little easier with some unconscious comic relief from Michael. The wait proved too difficult for him and he fell asleep on the conveyor belt that when operational, carried the luggage from the ferry to the shore. He had been sleeping soundly for about an hour when the conveyor started. He remained asleep as it carried him along the boardwalk toward the shore. He woke about five metres down the walkway and discovered that he was the cause of the laughter of the large crowd who had queued during his slumber. It was most certainly a welcome distraction from our tiredness. The 'get-togethers' were not just parties but special events. They were an integral part of being an exchange student and were much like a life compass. They were a haven for the creation and furthering of friendships and loves, a medium through which knowledge was shared and an opportunity to seek and give advice. They discreetly banished shyness and built confidence. They enabled mentees to become mentors and were nurseries for future leaders. The fact this aspect of the get-together was not immediately recognisable did not diminish its existence. The other aspect that was not immediately obvious to us, yet what was occurring was a metaphorical shrinking of our world. Despite the distances that would, in future, separate us, our experiences would forever keep us bound. In this regard, we were each a seed making the world an abundant garden of goodwill and international understanding for the other.

9

Marvellous Marselisborg

Fearful of forgetting any number of people who made my time at Marselisborg Gymnasium a most wondrous experience, I name them only by category. The understanding of the teachers, the friendship of the students from all grades and the assistance of the administration, all combined to ensure that my scholarship at Marselisborg Gymnasium was memorable beyond description. Every day seemed to be one adventure after another. It would be dishonest to say that there was never an ordinary school day – a handful of pages in my diary saying, "regular school day" or just, "school" would evidence that. In context, though, a regular school day on exchange is considerably more interesting than a regular school day at home. Even if that were not the case, the regular days numbered so few that they were nothing more than an aberration. There were also a number of extra special school events that I knew would continue to hold prominence in my memories of Denmark.

Despite having never studied Biology, nor any science subject for several years, I was invited to attend a Biology study tour. My Biology class, combined with another class in the same subject, set off for Lake Mossø, approximately 90 minutes' bicycle ride from Aarhus. My first host family had given me a bicycle early in my stay with them, which I also took to my subsequent families. It was a heavy bike with only three gears, which made the ride to Mossø seem longer than it would have been on my trusty 10-speed at home in Australia. The rain, which set in after only about ten kilometres, also seemed to add distance to the journey. It was only uncomfortable for the first few minutes – after that we all adapted. Adapting was something that I had become particularly good at, especially given it was a fundamental and regular aspect of exchange. Despite the rain and the heavy bike, the ride didn't pose any trouble for me at all. Mossø was a visually stunning place. The third largest freshwater lake in Denmark and home to all manner of wildlife, the time spent there was amazing.

We arrived at Mossø where we found our very basic timber cabins and unpacked our luggage and equipment. One of the teachers and one student had driven their cars loaded with our bags, equipment and food. Had we been required to take all of that on the bikes, then the ride would have posed a problem. A somewhat recurrent theme for me on exchange also applied to our Biology excursion – namely that time was precious. We didn't rest long before taking some containers to the water's edge in search of suitable samples of water, watergrass and tiny water insects. I had never been involved in such a subject nor the various projects that we were undertaking that afternoon. We examined the samples in our make-shift laboratory and tested the water. Our exact purpose wasn't entirely clear to me, but I was more than able to participate and assist my classmates.

The next day saw me assigned with Casper and Christina to take a small rowboat out onto the lake to obtain samples of the water from further out. As was all too often typical of the Danish weather, we were only just completing the required sampling when the sky clouded over and dumped heavy cold rain on us. So persistent was the rain, we could hardly see in which direction we were rowing. The positive side to that little adventure was that we were the first to hit the showers, which had managed to run out of hot water the night before before we were all finished.

The first night of our excursion was very quiet given that most of us were rather tired from the ride and from the various projects upon our arrival. In a night of stark contrast to that of our first, the second was most enjoyable and late. We all enjoyed a few beers over a game of Trivial Pursuit, played in teams due to the numbers present. Luckily for me, my team agreed to translate many of the questions, which proved quite difficult because of language, rather than content. This was particularly so for several unique or specialty words that I had not at that time encountered during the development of my ever-increasing Danish vocabulary.

In addition to the language barrier, I was distracted by the suggestive glances of two schoolmates: one from my own class and one from the other class. As the hour grew late and we finished our second game of Trivial Pursuit, I withdrew to my bedroom. As I opened the door, Mathilde tapped me on the shoulder and asked if she could come into my room. Not one to disappoint, I welcomed her in and got changed in her presence. No sooner had I changed, there was a knock at the door. It was Vilma, a girl from the other class on the excursion. She was wondering if I wanted a night-cap before bed. Before I had a chance to answer, Mathilde told her to go away, a direction not welcomed nor followed by Vilma. What followed was very embarrassing as I had never before had two girls argue over who might share the remaining hours of the night with me. How impossible it was when they both turned to me and asked me to decide! In hindsight, it seemed ludicrous to think that any type of diplomacy might work in such a situation, particularly given the distortions to reason caused by the numerous beers consumed by all three of us earlier that night. Whether it was a naive attempt at diplomacy, or a misconceived notion of harm minimisation, my response to the situation was to disappoint only one, not two. I figured it was the lesser of two evils to have Vilma disappointed with me. She wasn't actually from my class and I would not therefore have to be at odds with a classmate for the rest of the year. Mathilde was delighted that I made the decision for her to remain in my room. As a result, the rest of the night was most pleasant indeed, as she more than ably demonstrated that she was grateful.

I wasn't sure whether it was a matter of good planning or simply good luck, but breakfast wasn't scheduled until 9:00am the next day. Despite the leniency of our timetable, the late breakfast was hard to stomach; much harder, was the clean-up roster on which I was included. Nonetheless, we were all on time for our short bicycle ride to the eel farm some two kilometres away. Most of the students declined to handle the long slimy eels, citing both the smell of the enclosure and the perceived texture of the skin. I had handled eels before, so did not hesitate to take one into my hands when asked. Our guide proceeded to show us maps of the lake and highlighted the areas that were most populated by the eels. He sought to educate the group on the various environmental factors impacting upon both the lake and the habitat of the eels. The eel farm visit rounded out the end of our excursion and we all returned to our cabins. All was packed and we were ready to leave when I was made an offer I couldn't refuse. Mathilde's father had driven out to save her the ride home and she offered me the spare seat available. His car had bicycle racks that easily accommodated both our bikes and there was plenty of room for our luggage in the back. About halfway back, Mathilde's Dad said, "well, I hope Mathilde looked after you" in response to me telling him that I had never studied Biology. Indeed, she had looked after me, but there was no way that was going to be discussed further with him and in any event, Mathilde and I decided not to continue seeing each other.

I did study another science subject at Marselisborg Gymnasium, but it was at the very opposite end of the academic spectrum to Biology. It was Political Science and was a subject in which I took great interest. A study tour was planned for the subject and, again, I was welcomed along. This tour though, was considerably longer in both distance and time and could not be done on a bicycle. My Political Science class study tour was to Belgium. Given the enormity of my homeland, school excursions never crossed international borders. In fact, given the size of my home state, they only occasionally involved interstate travel. The geographical location of Denmark, however, lent itself to class excursions that quite commonly took on an international flavour. The school had given me advance notice of the impending tour and that enabled me to obtain the necessary visa, parental and Rotary permits.

We left the school very early on a Sunday morning and didn't see the sunshine until soon after we crossed the Danish/German border. The bus was certainly not as comfortable as that used on the Euro-Tour and after about five hours of travelling, it became evident that it was not as mechanically sound either. As we approached an overpass, we heard a loud bang followed by a violent shudder of the entire vehicle. The driver promptly parked the bus off the autobahn, just under the overpass. We were stranded for about one hour, which made for a very long day. I always looked for positives from the very few negative situations I encountered on exchange and although it wasn't fantastic, there was something to be taken from our breakdown. I joined a couple of friends from school and climbed to the top of the concrete incline under the overpass. We simply sat watching the passing traffic and talked as close friends can for any amount of time. It was nothing special for them, being very familiar with the autobahn, however, for me it actually had some appeal. I had heard about the German motorways and had experienced them a few times already on exchange. However, from my perch high above the road, I could better appreciate some of the very powerful cars and the great speeds at which they were travelling. Nearly all the cars were travelling at speeds that would simply never be seen on Australian roads – at least not legally. Once the mechanic arrived, he took little time identifying the problem and making the necessary repair. I was not certain of the explanation but understood it to be a blown fanbelt. Without further incident, we resumed our travel and arrived at our hostel in Brussels.

After travelling for so long, one could be excused for believing a good night's sleep would be the highest priority, but it was not. Instead, in typical Danish fashion, I enjoyed the company of my classmates until the early hours of the morning. It was rather cold and my classmates simply sat our abundant supply of Jupiler beer in the planter boxes on the outside of our windows. That was enough to keep them cold for drinking.

When due consideration was given to the indulgences the evening before, it made sense that breakfast was simply coffee, bread and jam. It seemed enough though, to sustain us through the morning's agenda at NATO headquarters. I had already experienced a small part of NATO – well at least one ship in the navy of one of the member nations – but to visit the organisation's headquarters was impressive. While I usually respected the law, I couldn't help but take a photo of the front gates to the NATO headquarters compound, upon which was a large sign indicating that photography was prohibited. We were met by some of the Danish representatives in NATO and shown around the facility. Following lunch, we met Danish members of the European Community and heard lectures on both the European and Danish economies and Denmark's responsibilities. Needless to say, a great deal of the lectures were lost on me by virtue of a less than comprehensive mastery of the technical economic and political terms communicated in Danish.

That evening in Brussels must rank high among my adventures in Europe. After a lovely group dinner with the teachers, some of the more adventurous among us decided to see the city by night. We visited a couple of bars, played pool and enjoyed some Stella Artois beer. We were well aware that our hostel closed its doors from 1:00am to 7:00am and that access was not available during that time. With that in mind and at some late hour, we decided we should make our way back. As we were doing so, cold drizzling rain started to fall and we found ourselves darting from shop awning to shop awning most of the way back.

We were not far from our hostel when we came across a girl huddled under a shop awning, sobbing openly. I initially thought that I would be the least equipped to communicate with her, professing only a sound knowledge of English and a reasonable fluency in Danish. As it turned out, I *was* the most equipped as she could only speak broken English or her mother tongue, Hungarian.

Once she calmed down, I was able to determine that she was also a student visiting with her school from Szekszárd in Hungary. She had become separated from her classmates and could not find her way back to her hotel. I had a local map and had recalled seeing her hotel in our travels – the opulence of the Palace Hotel was not easily forgotten. I suggested to my classmates that they return to the hostel, while I escorted Leonora back to her hotel. Although Leonora and I took a couple of wrong turns, we made it back to her hotel without too much hassle. To my great dismay, the show of kindness had resulted in time skipping away from me and it was 1:50am. Leonora sensed my concern and asked me what was wrong. I explained that I was now locked out of my hostel and wouldn't be able to access it again until 7:00am. She suggested that I spend what was left of the night in her room and return early to my hostel. It seemed like the most sensible option at the time, as I wouldn't have been able to get into the hostel anyway and the cold rain continued to fall. It was actually quite romantic, in a funny sort of way. Even though I sensed no danger, I was alert to the fact that I was with a person I didn't know, in a place I didn't know and was accordingly very wary of what I was doing.

The hotel room was far superior to those of our hostel and infinitely more comfortable. I was relieved to see that there were two beds in the room – a queen sized bed and a single bed and fancied that the single bed would be mine. However, Leonora was concerned that her teacher would see two beds slept in and seek an impossible explanation. Her alternative suggestion was as scary as it was seductive. Leonora's rationale for insisting I share the queen bed with her was that my presence would not be noticed. I would then be able to leave early in the morning with nobody else any the wiser. It was not as though any hot blooded, eighteen-year-old Australian male would not want to be in that position, but it was nonetheless slightly uncomfortable. We had language difficulties, so the last thing I wanted to do was argue over the sleeping arrangements. Leonora possessed exceptional beauty and I figured she would not have any ulterior motives for the sleeping arrangements she had imposed. I was wrong. Leonora was dressed in only a bra and underpants, while I had kept my singlet and boxer shorts on. We had been talking as best we could about how she had become detached from her class, where she came from and how it was that I was with a group of Danish classmates. Suddenly, Leonora propped herself up on one elbow, such that her long, silky soft brown hair fell lightly over her chest. She asked me if she could thank me for helping her earlier, to which I naively replied, "I thought you did." With a smoothness only challenged by that of her skin, Leonora leaned forward and pressed her appreciative lips against mine. Needless to say, it was an experience I was not prepared for, let alone expecting. In the end, we enjoyed very little sleep before we showered and I hurriedly made my way back to my hostel where I joined my classmates for breakfast.

My dearest friend Hanne was irate, having been worried terribly, while most of the boys saw the chivalrous side. It was actually fortuitous that I had stayed out that night, because serious discipline was being handed out to my classmates upon my return. Apparently, my friends had continued their debauchery and mischief at the hostel late into the night. I, for obvious reasons, was not subject to the teachers' scrutiny.

The evening was one that highlighted for me, the dynamics of risk and reward, choice and consequence. There were of course risks with the choices I made that night, but thankfully, in that instance, the consequence was reward. I had often wondered what the term street-smart meant or how one could become street-smart. In the days, weeks and months that followed that night in particular, I felt the meaning was presenting itself.

Our final full day in Brussels was largely spent attending more lectures. A highlight for me though, was that the featured lecture of the day was delivered in English, which allowed me to participate actively in the question-and-answer session. We were told about some of the more interesting recent activities of NATO in and around the European region. One such operation was called 'Operation Maritime Mentor', which was essentially a naval blockade in the international waters off the former Yugoslavia. This, we were told, was aimed at enforcing sanctions. It sparked in me a curiosity about a diplomatic career instead of the legal one planned. It seemed to me, that in a very small way, I was already an ambassador of Australian youth and, in that capacity, contributing to international peace and understanding. The thought of doing that as a career was appealing. On our final evening in Brussels, only a few beers were consumed and we simply sat around talking. This was probably a combination of us all being very tired and the berating my classmates had received that morning.

Early the next morning, I enjoyed breakfast with my classmates and teachers before helping with the tidy up, and loading of the bus. I was not, however, returning to Denmark with my class. Instead, I was realising plans made, some weeks prior, to visit a classmate from my school in Australia. My departure from Brussels wasn't until lunchtime and I had been excused from attending the last of the lectures, so I had several hours free to do as much or as little as I wished. It was some day of celebration, or at least locally so in Brussels. I decided to walk around the city for a short while and take in some nearby sights that I hadn't previously seen. The Cinquantenaire Park was very impressive even though the weather was poor, and was largely absent the colour it would normally enjoy in summer. Standing ever so prominently in the middle of the park was the famous triumphal arch, construction of which started in 1880 and took over twenty years to complete. My class had, earlier in our tour, driven past the Berlaymont Building, which was home to the European Commission

Headquarters. It was a distinctive building, and I wanted to find it again for the unique photo opportunity it presented. As I wandered, I happened upon a very large military marching band with an even larger regiment of soldiers following behind. There were thousands of people lining the streets, and I felt rather crowded. I had my backpack and a suitcase and being mindful of contingencies, decided to make my way to the train station.

Train stations can be boring places, but in this instance, it was a warm and dry safe haven, where I could escape the cold and wet conditions outside and simply rest up. I had to catch three trains in total, with transfers at Cologne and Oberhausen, before ultimately arriving in Hünxe. Strangely, those three train journeys, and the necessary transfers between them, didn't feel that foreign to me despite not understanding a word of German. I was in a foreign country, hearing a foreign language and passing through foreign towns, but again, it didn't feel foreign. As the colours and shapes of the German landscape flashed in and out of view from the window of the train, I actually pondered that phenomenon. It felt obvious to me. I could only conclude that in becoming Danish, I was also, in a small way, becoming European. I was for that time at least, part of that culturally rich community of nations known as Europe.

Once I arrived, I telephoned Andrew who came with his host mother to collect me. The remainder of the day was spent catching up with Andrew and getting to know his host family, who were just lovely. Andrew had been having a wonderful year and was well established with his host family and with his school. The school was considerably larger than mine in Denmark, both in terms of its campus and the student population. Many of the buildings were reasonably new and modern. Because the campus was comprised of several detached buildings, there was far more landscaping in the common areas between them. Andrew too, was a former Miami High School graduate and had embarked on a ten-month exchange to Germany. He wasn't with Rotary and had just one family for the duration of his stay. Exchange through his organisation was vastly different than those through the Rotary Youth Exchange Program. The shorter duration and the one host family for the entire time, were obvious differences. I discovered, though, from my discussions with Andrew, that there were more alarming differences. By comparison, the support network I enjoyed with Rotary was virtually non-existent with his organisation. As a result, such amazing experiences as the Euro-Tour and the student 'get-togethers' were arranged on a mostly ad hoc basis and almost entirely by the students themselves. More importantly though, there were very limited opportunities to seek out and receive emotional support and counselling should it have been needed. They were assigned area managers who may have been responsible for up to 15 or 20 students in their area. In Rotary, we had a club counsellor in both our sponsoring club at home and, of course, our hosting club. Usually, such counsellors would only be responsible for one or two students at any given time. Beyond all of that was the fact that Rotary was a large global humanitarian organisation that did much more than only youth exchange. Among the similarities, though, was the intensity with which life as an exchange student was lived. The exposure to wonderful and exciting experiences, the challenges and the personal growth that comes was virtually the same.

The next day at Andrew's school was simply sensational. His class and his teachers were very accepting of my attendance and asked me to speak with them about my exchange in Denmark. It was with immense pride for Denmark and gratitude for my life in that country, that I spoke so highly of my experiences as an exchange student. I reflected later that the passion and pride with which I spoke of Denmark was further evidence still that Denmark had become very much a part of who I was, and I was sure, always would be. We lunched that day in a nearby mall and I became quite friendly with one of Andrew's classmates. Mia had a presence about her, an intangible aura of self-confidence and beauty. She naturally commanded attention yet was sincere enough not to thrive on it. Her voice was almost musical and her smile so alluring. Andrew had assured me that Mia would not be romantically interested in a visitor, someone who would, in a week, be gone from her life. It was apparent though, that when two people were so naturally attracted, the future seemed of little importance and had no bearing on the moment. Mia had been on exchange in the United States the previous year and was well aware of the reality in which we found ourselves. We both knew that our time together would only ever be a short, but ever so special encounter.

There was another Australian exchange student living in Andrew's town, and she came from Melbourne. Katherine, Andrew and I spent a very long day travelling on several trains to nearby Luxembourg. Although a small country, landlocked and bordered by Germany, Belgium and France, it was steeped in history and importance. It had become home to many of the European Community departments, including one of the three seats of the European Parliament. Walking only a distance of a few hundred metres, we were exposed to thousands of years of history. The extraordinary Petrusse Valley, with both the Bock and Petrusse Casemates dating back to 1644, was simply amazing. The casemates were exceptional examples of a military fortification that spanned hundreds of years. It was yet another UNESCO World Heritage listed site visited and the only one in Luxembourg. The famous 'Old Bridge' standing some 45 metres above the valley would not have been out of place on that list. The 24 arches supported the span of some 290 metres and had stood proudly for over 130 years. In my view though, the most amazing site was the Quirinus Chapel. It was an old pilgrimage chapel built into the solid rock face of the valley in 1355. There were really only two disappointments from the visit – namely the weather and the equally poor attitude of the locals toward visitors. It was a distinctly obvious difference to the experiences I had enjoyed almost everywhere else in Europe. Perhaps the locals we encountered were having a bad day, but almost all were not in the least bit welcoming or even helpful. It didn't matter though, as we thoroughly enjoyed each other's company as we trekked all over the historic city. We arrived back to Andrew's home well after dark and had only enough energy to climb the stairs and go to bed.

Perhaps it was adolescent naivety, or maybe it was true mutual affection, but I had really missed Mia the day before. My feelings were shared by Mia as she ran up and gave me a huge hug when I arrived at school the next day. Our flourishing friendship had been a somewhat private affair up to that point. We decided to visit a local nightspot that evening, and Mia arrived early to pick Andrew and me up from his house. Before the club, we went to a church group viewing of the movie *Dances With Wolves*. It was dubbed in German and, as a result, I understood nothing. Mia and I stepped out for a large part of the movie to spend some time together. We returned at the end of the movie to pick up Andrew, Katherine and one of Mia's friends. The nightspot was a great venue for dancing and playing pool, both of which we did extensively, before returning home about 1:00am. Andrew ventured inside the moment we arrived home, but Mia asked me to spend some more time with her in the car. We realised just how close we were that night and demonstrated those feelings to each other. I finally snuck into Andrew's home and went to bed at about 2:30am. Although I went to bed late, I was up early with Andrew to attend my last day with him at his German school. Soon after arriving, Mia asked me to take a drive with her. I obliged, not knowing where we were going, but soon discovered that our destination was her house. Both her parents were at work for the day and Mia wanted to spend quality time with me in private and in considerably greater comfort than in the car the evening before. It was exciting, it was beautiful and it was four hours of my time in Germany that I knew would forever rank highly among my memories of that country. In fact, after those four hours, I actually believed I was in love. As natural an emotion as it was, love in that sense was a most dangerous feeling to be held by an exchange student. The next day, when I had to say goodbye not only to Andrew but also to Mia, I realised just how dangerous. Mia's tears soaked my shirt as we embraced on the platform of the train station, bidding each other a long goodbye. We vowed to meet again, either in Germany or in Denmark. As the winter sun set in the sky above, I sensed, though, it also set metaphorically on what was a short but sweet relationship with my German love. While my memories of Mia and the time that we had shared were not nearly as beautiful as she was, they were all I had to take with me. Yet again on my extraordinary journey, I had been vulnerable to the joy and excitement of love, only to be strengthened by the necessity of leaving it behind.

My train trip from Germany back to Denmark was a lonely and devastating one. Fresh from a wonderfully busy week with friends and new-found love, over ten hours alone on a train had a very sobering effect – almost depressingly so. I spoke little of my train trip from Germany and recorded even less of it in my diary. There were three reasons for this, one of which was the mischievous nature by which I held my ticket, the second because of what happened to me and the third, because I didn't want to re-live the events in writing or at all. Katherine's father had recently visited her in Germany and had left behind his first-class Euro-rail pass that still had three days to run. It was probably the wrong thing to do, but my sense of adventure was such that I accepted the ticket, and I boarded the train in the first class section. The obvious risk was not apparent to me until the train ground to a halt at the border between Germany and Denmark and customs officers boarded the train. I felt a chilling cold rush through my body as I realised the dilemma I would be in if the customs officer and the ticket collector attended upon me at once. The first-class Euro-rail ticket had the name of a doctor, Katherine's father, printed on it and clearly the name on my passport was different. While my passport was checked, my rail ticket was fortunately not checked at all over the trip, so I was lucky in that sense.

My reluctance to remember the train trip stemmed not so much from the ticket adventure, but from a misadventure on the Hamburg railway platform while I was waiting for a connecting train. It was late, I was well dressed and quite laden with luggage, having been on tour for some two weeks. Despite the Hamburg train station being the busiest train station in all of Germany and one of the busiest in Europe, I was mostly alone on the platform. There were people around but either on other platforms or a fair distance away in the station itself. Because I was travelling in the first-class cabins, I was waiting at the very end of the designated platform, which made my isolation more pronounced. Other than a dirty brown mouse with rather matted hair and an unusually long tail, I was very much alone and certainly felt that way. As I watched the little rodent run along the lines between the tiles on the platform floor as though it was following some route on a road map, my mind wandered. Sadness pervaded my thoughts, although I wasn't entirely sure why. I was tired. It appears that in that condition, I was like honey to a bee for two undesirable characters of very little human worth.

Their assault on me was not only random and violent but their intentions particularly devious. One was grabbing at my belt, while the other had already loosened his to expose himself. If there was anything fortunate about the incident, it was that my attackers were not particularly strong nor dexterous. The one attempting to loosen my belt was also the one who had grabbed me by the throat and pulled me backwards off the wooden bench seat. He couldn't maintain his hold around my neck and loosen my belt at the same time. Added to that was the fact that the adrenalin was flowing fast through my veins, which saw me react with the speed of a pouncing panther and the result was that I was a bit too hard to handle. My reaction was not what saved me though. No, my saviour actually took the form of a short old platform guard, who came running to my rescue. No doubt he had heard my screams for help, and the sounding of his whistle was enough to send the cowardly attackers running. They ran across some tracks and up a grassed verge nearby and quickly disappeared from view. The guard's tired eyes, hardened by the passing of time and seemingly held in place by wrinkled eyelids, were at the same time so soft, as he extended his hand to help me to my feet. I understood nothing he said, nor he my words of thanks and gratitude, but I don't think the message was lost. He seemed to query whether I wanted him to call the police, but I didn't. I simply wanted to go home. Although shocked and shaken, I was fine, and still had enough awareness to remember the circumstances of my first-class ticket. I had lost nothing but a bit of dignity and my kindly saviour sat with me until my connecting train arrived some ten minutes later. Beyond my parents, I had rarely used the term 'hero' to describe anyone. In that unfamiliar place and in those unfamiliar circumstances, sat an unknown individual whom I regarded as my hero.

Denmark had felt like home from very early in my stay and stepping onto the Aarhus station platform after that trip was certainly no exception. Truly, it had never felt more like home. Outwardly, there was very little sign of what I had experienced, except perhaps for the slightly swollen and blackened eye and a small cut to my lip. Both of these were easily attributed to a fabricated fight over a game of pool while in Germany. I figured that people can't control their destiny, it is predetermined and intangible. I reasoned that people do, however, have free choice. The choice of what to eat, the clothes to wear and the sports they would follow and most importantly, a choice in dealing with events of the past. I had just spent several hours travelling alone by train between Hamburg and Aarhus. It had given me more than enough time to contemplate these things and decide my course. I chose to deal with it immediately by discounting it as an unfortunate case of being in the wrong place at the wrong time. I determined that if I did not deal with it in that way, then I would have had to recount the experiences to my host family, to my family at home, to my counsellor and possibly others in an official capacity. I asked myself whether this would reverse what had happened. Of course, it would not. I asked myself if it would remove the hurt and erase the memory. Of course, it would not. I asked myself could any good come from such disclosure. Of course, there could not. Everything about my exchange was so wonderful, in every other respect. Sure, what had happened on that station platform was horrible, but I had so much more to be thankful for and didn't want to waste one further moment of time dealing with that negative. I knew I had many more great memories to create and that would be my focus. In its own strange way, I knew that the experience would influence my perspectives and add to my character. It certainly added to my resilience in the face of challenges.

Most of my teachers expressed some excitement at having me in their class but none more so than Birthe, my English teacher. She was a friendly teacher, conversant with much of classic English literature and with the rules of grammar and usage. I had long been fascinated at how capable my classmates were with my mother tongue and the academic demands placed upon them in the subject of English were equally amazing. I saw it as both humorous and challenging when Birthe returned a written paper to me with minor corrections and comments. She was so genuinely pleased to have me in her class and saw me as an opportunity to help promote interest in her subject. I was learning from them and, in that subject more than in any other, they were learning from me.

Birthe had organised an excursion for the English classes of the school, which involved a trip to Copenhagen. She was insistent that I also attend. It had been an extremely busy month, started off by the tour of Brussels, Germany and Luxembourg, only to end with yet more travel. It didn't take much persuasion, though, as I welcomed the chance to again visit the nation's capital. We travelled by bus and ferry, both modes of transport I was familiar with. The ferry was one of the most popular modes of transport between Aarhus and Copenhagen given the geographical location of Aarhus on the harbour. In order to keep costs to a minimum, it was necessary, on this three-day excursion, to arrange our own accommodation. Bendt's relatives lived in Copenhagen, and they welcomed me for the duration of the visit. I thoroughly enjoyed myself, as I could sight-see like a tourist, yet remain under the guise of a Danish high school student. Perhaps the highlight of the excursion was our visit to DR Television, which is the main television station for Denmark. We were given guided tours of the station and I even got to play newsreader for a moment as I took up position behind a nightly news desk. The admiration I felt from my classmates was elevated to a whole new level when I sat myself down beside Tommy Troelsen in the cafeteria during one of our lunch breaks. Tommy, too, was having lunch with colleagues and was spotted by a few of my peers. I had previously met Tommy when holidaying with Carl and Marie at Himmerland and was immediately remembered by him. I invited him over to meet my classmates, and they were very appreciative of him doing so. They were of course, perplexed at how I, as a foreigner, could know Tommy on such a personal level. Again, my English teacher was most pleased with my involvement.

One of our days in Copenhagen was a free day do to with what we wished. I decided to catch the train north to the town of Helsingør and visit Kronborg Slot, which is more popularly known as Hamlet's castle. Helsingør itself was little more than a fishing village, but its proximity on the coast of the strait between Denmark and Sweden ensured that it developed into an important Danish centre. I learned that centuries prior, when Denmark controlled the southern parts of Sweden, the King had imposed a toll for all foreign ships seeking to pass through that strategically important strait. He had also built fortifications on the opposing coasts of the strait – in Helsingør and in its close Swedish neighbour town of Helsingborg. However, Helsingør was arguably most well-known because of its part in one of the most celebrated plays in English literature. Known virtually the world over, Shakespeare's tale of Hamlet, the Prince of Denmark, was set in Helsingør and, more particularly, in Kronborg castle. Indeed, over the years, the Shakespearean play had been performed at the castle countless times. Such famous actors as Richard Burton, Michael Redgrave and the legendary Laurence Olivier had assumed the title role of Hamlet in performances on-site at Kronborg.

Often on exchange, I would take the time to discover places on my own. With time being very much at a premium, though, I took a guided tour of the castle. I was thankful for the tour, because it taught me that the castle's origins as a military fortification rendered it unsuitable as a Royal residence, at least to the Renaissance standards of that time. As a result, King Frederik II started modernising the medieval castle in 1574, just two years after marrying his young cousin, Sofie of Mecklenburg. It took just over ten years to complete the works, turning the castle into a spectacular Royal residence comprised of four multi-storey wings, oriel towers on the outer corners, octagonal stair turrets facing the courtyard and a copper roof with stunning decorative gables. The addition of large moats around the castle and a magnificent water fountain in the middle of it, also occurred during this renaissance period for the castle. Almost one hundred years later, the castle again became a military base from which the Dano-Swedish wars were fought and, not surprisingly, it suffered great damage during this time. It continued to serve as a military barracks until 1924, at which time the castle was once more restored. With such a rich and diverse history, it was easy to understand why it enjoyed significant prominence among the finest castles of Northern Europe.

Under the castle was an extensive system of casemates. It was cold, damp and dark, but an absolute must on the list of things to experience at Kronborg. I chuckled to myself as I made my way through the casemates, remembering the question asked of me in my interview for exchange. Here I was in a cold, dark castle. Sitting famously in those casemates was a large statue of Holger Danske. Holger the Dane was an important national symbol for generations of Danish people, and it was wonderful to see. Such was the importance of Holger Danske to the Danish people, that during the German occupation of Demark from 1940 to 1945, one of the most significant resistance cells operated under that name. Born of legend, the story as it was told to me, was that if ever the kingdom of Denmark was threatened by a foreign enemy, the great stone figure would come to life and defend his country. Interestingly the legend of Holger Danske originated not in Denmark, but in medieval French literature, as one of Charlemagne's great Danish warriors. Equally as interesting was the fact that the imposing concrete statue had been first cast in plaster, as a mould for the striking of a bronze statue commissioned by a local hotel in 1907. The damp climate of the casemates under Kronborg was damaging to the plaster cast, so it was re-cast in concrete less than ten years before I visited.

I could have easily explored Kronborg castle for the entire day, but I still wanted to see some other sights. One of those sights was the twin town to Helsingør, namely Helsingborg in Sweden. The strait between Denmark and Sweden at that location was called Øresund and was a stretch of water only about five kilometres wide. There was a regular ferry service with departures every 15 minutes or so and the entire journey took less than half an hour. I thought it would be a good opportunity to visit another country and embarked on yet another trip. I boarded the ferry and made my way to an outdoor seating section on the boat. It was a fine day, which enabled me to see clear to Sweden. The ferry ride was comfortable, but lonely, as I was the only passenger sitting outside. It had not occurred to me, until walking into the ferry terminal, that I would require a passport. I had not taken it with me to Copenhagen as I was on a school excursion and the trip to Sweden was very much on impulse. Most salient in my mind, though, was the feeling of being Danish. So, I chose boldly to continue and walked straight past the customs officer, showing him only the nod of my head, while wishing him a good morning in Danish. It turned out to be no problem at all and I spent the day enjoying the city of Helsingborg.

Just as Kronborg was the most visited site in Helsingør, so too was Kärnan, a medieval castle tower located high on the hills above Helsingborg harbour. It was a most intriguing experience to explore a Swedish landmark and learn that not only the building, but the entire region around it was once controlled by the Danes. Indeed, it was that absorbing history between Denmark and Sweden that had so fundamentally impacted upon the tower. Centuries before, the tower was the centrepiece to a much larger fortification. It had once boasted a large hall building, fourteen semi-circular towers and a defensive brick wall that measured 150 metres in circumference. However, following the devastating Scanian wars fought between Denmark and Sweden, as well as the passage of time, the tower was all that remained. I ventured some thirty-five metres up the narrow spiralling staircase to the summit of the tower and was exposed to the most magnificent view of the harbour, the strait and Denmark in the distance.

I didn't for a minute think that I would have to worry about my passport when returning to Denmark. After all, I had, in my mind at least, become Danish and was simply returning home. I was wrong. As I approached the customs official, I offered him the same courtesy I had given the Swedish officer earlier in the day, however, met with a very different response. He was very matter of fact and asked me to produce my passport for inspection. I explained that I was an exchange student and was returning from a day trip to Sweden. He took me to the office where he proceeded to check my credentials and my story. It took little more than a telephone call to my host family in Aarhus to prove I was who I said I was and he let me through with only a warning.

The remainder of my daytrip was without incident, and I returned in time to join with my classmates at the theatre. Coincidentally, we were attending a dinner performance of Shakespeare's famous play, *Hamlet*. Even though it was performed in Danish, I understood much of the play, enhanced perhaps by the fact that I had only hours earlier, been surrounded by the very setting for the story.

Football is one of the more popular of Danish sports and I found myself quite enjoying the spectacle. I had often been asked by the boys from not only my class but the school generally, whether football was popular in Australia. The answer was never simple and, more often than not, resulted in a lengthy dialogue on how Australia has a number of different codes of football. It would also invariably result in the giving of my personal preference for Rugby League and an explanation of the game. On one occasion, I was challenged with the proposition that Rugby League was not as tough or as entertaining as American Football. The source for this proposition were the boys who had been on exchange in the United States and had played it at the high school level. The debate was healthy and productive. The product of the debate was an undertaking from the boys to organise a hybrid game of American Football and Rugby League. Surprisingly, agreement on the new rules for this hybrid game was not that difficult to achieve. The rules of note abandoned from American Football were that there would be no separate attacking and defensive teams, the game would consist of two forty-minute halves, each uninterrupted by breaks and the football had to be placed on the ground over the try-line as opposed to a touch-down. Conversely, the rules incorporated into the ordinary Rugby League rules were that twice in any given set of six tackles, a player could throw a forward pass, such as the downfield throws seen in American Football. Players could also block and shield other players, although not take them out of play. Given the number of interested players, the on-field numbers were extended from thirteen to fifteen, with an interchange of players limited to six. A date was set and the teams were allocated. I told Matthew about the arrangement, and he was keen to add another Aussie to my playing ranks.

The game was set for a Monday, so Matthew came to stay with me on the preceding Saturday morning. Together we trained our team on the strategies and skills required for the epic encounter. The school wholly endorsed the experiment, extending the lunch break as necessary to accommodate the two hours required to prepare, play and clean up afterwards. They even supplied some drinks and light refreshments. The other students, too, rallied in support, and banners were even made and hung on the fences. The toughness of the game took Matthew and me by surprise. However, the biggest surprise came when Matthew and I ran out from the change rooms, wearing only our shoes, socks, shorts and shirt. The other boys almost unanimously had shoulder pads, shin pads and three even wore the American Football helmets they had souvenired from America. Given the obvious dangers, it was agreed they would not wear the helmets. The crowd was actually very large. It was made up of other students, teachers, administration staff and even some family and friends of the players. The school photographer was in attendance, as was one from the local newspaper. The air of expectation was great, and I actually took a moment to ponder what it was I had created. We had a student who took on multiple roles of timekeeper, referee and scorekeeper, who despite an obvious lack of ready knowledge of the rules, tried to control the more serious infringements such as head-high tackles that had been outlawed. It was also his job to keep score and keep track of the number of tackles made.

The kick-off not only rocketed the ball deep into the opposition territory, it also signalled the commencement of the supporters' cheers and jeers. The first five or so minutes were played at an astonishing pace, with two tries for each side. There were no goal posts and no real substitute, so instead we modified the rules around conversions after a try. Following a try, the try-scorer would have to attempt to kick the ball into the football goals that were moved into place after each try. Of course, kicking a Rugby League ball along the ground or in the air in an effort to land it within the goals was very challenging. After those early minutes, however, the players started to get a feel and understanding for the game being played and the scoring slowed considerably.

The conclusion of the first half saw my team in front by ten points, but down one player. Lasse had been hit hard in a two-man tackle about two minutes out from half time. He had fallen awkwardly and, with the weight of two tacklers, had broken his ankle. At the time, we knew he was in terrific pain but didn't know why. His terribly swollen ankle was a fair indicator, so an ambulance was called to take him to hospital at which time the unfortunate diagnosis was made. Thankfully, that was the only serious injury, although I joined with a player from the other side in suffering a bloody nose. It was hard to police head-high tackles, particularly when the concept was quite new to all the players. A stray forearm had collected my face. At one point in the game, I ran onto a fantastic pass from Matthew who had broken the defensive line. I was frequently able to carry a tackler or two, but as I approached the try-line ball in hand, I was determined to cross it. I ended up scoring the try with four opposition players piled on top of me. I deserved less credit than I received, as tackling was not something my classmates were used to doing. They were especially unfamiliar with tackling around the legs, which enabled me to continue driving forward. The game was a resounding success with my team building on its half time score to finish at 34 - 18. More importantly, all those present unreservedly agreed that League was a far harder game to play than American Football. I had long been comfortable in the role of ambassador for Australian youth and a representative of Rotary Youth Exchange, but it seemed I could also add ambassador for Rugby League.

Quite apart from the academic and cultural lessons learned at Marselisborg Gymnasium, it was the interaction between all facets of Danish education that made it enjoyable. There were several parties held on campus, and these were very different from what I had always known to be a school dance. Schools at home would, from time to time, have school dances, but they were rather heavily policed for contraband such as cigarettes and alcohol. This was one of the many stark contrasts I observed during my time at Marselisborg Gymnasium. Students at school parties in Denmark were at liberty to smoke and drink as they wished. There were several parties held on campus throughout the year, but one particularly enjoyable party was jungle themed. The entire student and staff population worked tirelessly throughout Friday afternoon to decorate the main dining hall and stage area, as well as the hallways and part of the exterior of the building. There was the jungle-green coloured military camouflage netting, real and fake trees brought in and even stuffed animals placed around the rooms. Of course, everyone attended in costume, some more authentically 'jungle' than others. Among the jungle activity, I bumped into Mathilde from my Biology class. We danced for a while before escaping the jungle for an empty classroom, undecorated and unused. It was the first opportunity I'd had to spend some time with her since the Biology tour. My diary had been so full with other school, and non-school, travel that we hadn't been able to get together again. But those couple of hours signalled the start of more regular contact over the weeks that followed and forever changed the way I would view that classroom. The teachers, too, participated actively in the social aspects of Marselisborg. Not only would they enthusiastically attend functions at the school, but most would also host a gathering or two at their homes over the course of a year. Students would enjoy a dinner, drinks and music in teachers' homes. This was a very striking difference between Australian and Danish school culture. Much of my scholarship at Marselisborg Gymnasium epitomised the true nature of exchange. I learned so much from not only my teachers, but also from my classmates. Importantly, they were learning from me too. While much of the focus of exchange is on the exchange student, the number of lives positively touched is enormous. When all things were considered, I found Marselisborg Gymnasium to be a wonderfully special place of learning, life-long friendships and for me, cultural understanding.

10

Aarhus The City

Aarhus was known as the harbour city, which was hardly surprising given its position on the Aarhus Harbour. Along the coastline, many industries reliant upon the ocean, such as shipping, fishing and transport, had been established. A number of the enterprises were world renowned, including the Maersk Shipping Line, which would dock thousands of ships annually. There was a yacht club, which was perhaps the most contrasting feature of Aarhus come the winter months. It was a hive of activity in the summer with an abundance of colour, sunshine and people. Small to medium sized pleasure craft would sail in and out of the harbour and the yacht club with surprising frequency. The dining areas during the summer months commanded advanced bookings, because the food was as appealing as the outlook. In the winter months, though, virtually all that activity ceased. The only colour was varying shades of grey and to see a person walking around was rare indeed. Despite being the second largest city in Denmark, Aarhus was a small city by international standards. It did, however, boast the characteristics of a much larger one. It had several tourist attractions, an international atmosphere, a rich history and a fascinating culture. The people, though, really made the city great and were the reason for my becoming part of it.

Further along the coastline, Mother Nature imposed her presence, as industry and development thinned out and disappeared. Replacing buildings and docks, the Marselisborg forest rose splendidly out of the landscape. There are few places in this wide world of ours where a person can be completely at one with nature and yet still close to the city. The Marselisborg forest in summer was one such sanctuary. Obviously, if one were to visit the Amazon or other jungle of that magnitude, an indisputable closeness to nature would be experienced. However, the existence of such a reserve only minutes from the City of Aarhus reminded me of the geography of my city of birth. The Gold Coast boasted some of the world's best beaches, yet within an hour's drive, one could enjoy some of the lushest rainforest imaginable. Similarly, there were – in addition to the Marselisborg forest – a number of other equally beautiful forests within the Aarhus area. Locals and visitors alike would spend many hours exploring the forests that bordered the coastline. I spent a lot of time doing just that.

Towards the edge of the Marselisborg forest was Moesgaard Museum. Established in 1970, the museum was a very popular attraction. There were thousands of exhibits that traced the history of Denmark from the Stone Age to the Viking Age. Perhaps the most famous exhibit was the Grauballe Man. Preserved in every intricate detail by the organic matter in a nearby bog was the corpse of a human male. It was estimated that he was over 2000 years old, which meant he lived sometime during the Iron Age. He was found in 1952 at the village of Grauballe, some forty kilometres from Aarhus. Scientists have determined that he died from having his throat cut and, from the absence of calluses on his hands, that he was not a manual worker. Other injuries believed to have been inflicted at the time of his death further suggested that his death was a violent one. Outside the museum, a pathway passed through the woods and meadows with reconstructed examples of prehistoric dwellings, graveyards and villages. While I had never before been overly excited by museums, I found myself visiting and enjoying it many times.

Aarhus itself was very old, but the urban sprawl had seen the development of many new suburbs to the north, south and west of the city centre. There were buildings in Aarhus that were senior by age to the discovery of my homeland itself. Construction of the Cathedral in the heart of the city, for example, commenced in 1201. Several Renaissance buildings still stood throughout the city such as Juul's House, from 1629. Around the same time that the British discovered Australia, the Moesgård Manor House was being completed. Built in a neo-classical architectural style, this was an impressive building. Designed around a large courtyard, the main building boasted a basement, two floors and an attic level. Even though the building was placed on the Danish register of protected buildings in 1918, it was nonetheless a terrific testament to the builders that it was still standing all those years later.

Standing prominently in the heart of the city was Town Hall. With a towering timepiece reaching many storeys into the Aarhus skyline, it was an attraction that demanded attention. The clock tower was equipped with large bells at the top that chimed on the hour, every hour. On its face was a large clock, which measured some seven metres in diameter. The structure was clad with Norwegian marble and despite being more than fifty years old, was a remarkably modern looking building. During the summer months, the tourist bureau housed within Town Hall took guided tours to the tower-top belfry. The view of the City was without comparison and I enjoyed the experience greatly. While the appearance of the building was reasonably modern, the elevator was from the distant past. It was key operated and accessed through heavy wrought iron gates, had a panelled-timber floor, old mahogany wall timbers and massive brass buttons to select the chosen level. It clanged and banged its way from the ground level to the top of the tower some sixty metres above. It was not particularly large but was particularly slow. Ultimately, it served its purpose and took me to the top of the tower on more than one occasion during those summer months.

My frequent visits to the tourist bureau saw a friendship develop with the manager. Ingrid was a young lady, but I guessed several years older than me. She was intensely proud of the city for which she worked and always appeared happy to see me. On one of my numerous visits, I was wearing my Rotary jacket adorned in all its glory with my many badges and pins. Ingrid thought the jacket was wonderful and gave me an Aarhus City pin to add to my collection. Such a simple gift, but one she was not compelled to give. Furthermore, it perfectly complemented two other pins that held pride of place high on the lapel of my jacket. One was the city pin of the nation's capital, Copenhagen and the other, a crown-shaped pin featuring the Danish flag at its centre. While it wouldn't have looked nearly as impressive as it did, my jacket would have been complete with only those three important pins.

Soon after that visit, I made a special trip back to the tourist bureau and to Ingrid. That visit was not to go up the clock tower or to find further information about Aarhus or Denmark, but to simply thank Ingrid. I had arranged to take her for coffee, at which time I gave her some souvenir pins from Australia, one of my small souvenir koalas and other Aussie gifts. She was quite taken by this gesture, and I knew I had made yet another good friend in Denmark.

Late in my exchange year, I had access to a video camera and wanted to capture as much of Aarhus City on film as I could. It wouldn't have been the same if I had not been able to record the aerial view of the city that was so perfectly provided by the clock tower. Despite the chilling cold and wind, the weather was excellent. I had two visiting exchange students staying with me, and I thought it would be nice if they too could see the wonder of my city from that vantage point. Ingrid had certainly performed many favours for me over the preceding ten months, but this was a huge ask. The tower-top was closed in the winter months and no visitors were permitted at all. My request was made even more difficult by the fact that I had two other exchange students to take with me, and I was about to capture the experience on film. I was deeply appreciative when she bent the rules for me and escorted me, Michael and Angela once more to the top of the tower. Quite apart from any bureaucratic justification for the winter closure, the chilling cold proved a most persuasive proposition against winter visits. While frightfully cold, the view was still worth every moment as we recorded on film that which we would cherish for the rest of our lives – Aarhus. Michael and Angela were as suitably impressed by my ability to gain access to the out-of-season attraction as they were with the view.

Bisecting the City centre was Strøget, a long pedestrian mall which ran about 850 metres north from the Aarhus train station to the Cathedral. There were restaurants, banks, offices, a cinema and various types of shops located down either side of the mall. Scattered along its length, in the middle of the mall, were small food stalls selling fast food. Most famously, the stalls sold røde pølse, which was basically a type of boiled red sausage served in a hot dog roll, with a smorgasbord of sauces and condiments.

The pedestrian mall and surrounding laneways were also home to the city's annual festival known as Festuge or Festival Week. It took place over nine days in early September and had done so since 1965. Festuge was an amazing event full of colour, creativity, music and activity with a different theme each year. In 1992, it was *Det Ny Europa* meaning The New Europe, and I attended many times throughout the week. Not surprisingly, the busiest times of Festuge were the Friday and Saturday evenings. The mall on those nights was transformed into an ocean of people singing, dancing, eating, drinking and generally enjoying the live bands, other performers and exhibitions on display.

Adjacent to the Cathedral was an old 'hammer-and-bell' activity set up for the duration of the week. It involved a person swinging a large hammer-type tool onto a knob at the base of a tall structure sending a metal ball up the tower to a bell. If the hit was hard enough, the metal ball would cause the bell at the top to chime. The operator of the activity was able to achieve that result repeatedly, however, most of the participants could not. There were various prizes, depending on how many consecutive chimes one could achieve, from free beers to flowers. It was obvious to me, having swung an axe many times before, that the method most were using was their biggest impediment. I stood by as men much larger than me approached the task and failed. They would pick up the hammer, which was quite heavy, swing it up, over and behind their heads and then bring it straight back down again. This method was clumsy in that all the momentum from the upward swing was lost when having to swing it back over the head on the downward swing. I used a standard wood chopping swing, whereby the hammer was swung from in front of the body, around the side, up, over and down all in one movement. Therefore, the full power of the swing was realised as the momentum was not interrupted during the swing.

At the time of Festuge, I was still particularly friendly with Mathilde from my Biology class. Not surprisingly, the Friday night was spent with her, and it was in her company that I won several beers at the hammer-and-bell. Unfortunately, as the evening unfolded, I discovered I was being played. Mathilde actually had a much older boyfriend and, hand-in-hand, we stumbled across him in the crowd. He was an immigrant to Denmark, was in his early thirties and had a terribly short temper. Mathilde insisted to her boyfriend that we were only friends and that she was simply showing me around a very busy city. The situation was delicate, and despite all concerned having consumed several drinks, we were able to avoid any ugly scenes. What it did ensure – for me at least – was that from that point forward, we would indeed only be friends.

My participation in Festuge the following night was very much a solo act. At least it started out that way when I arrived in the city around 4:30pm. Michael was also visiting the city to experience Festuge and had overheard some locals talking about the Aussie on the hammer-and-bell. Because of my success on that attraction the night before, I had returned for more success and more free flowers and beer. Given that I was alone, I was winning flowers and handing them out among the girls in the crowd. I certainly didn't intend to give them to girls with boyfriends, especially after the episode with Mathilde's boyfriend the night before. As much as it wasn't my intention, it did happen a couple of times, but my immediate apology in both cases was enough for their boyfriends. I was pleased to see Michael arrive, and we then spent the rest of the night enjoying Festuge together. Friday night had ended on a slightly sour note, but Saturday night's enjoyment was sadly shattered by tragedy. At one point, the pedestrian mall crossed over a roadway several metres below. While Michael and I were sitting at a food stand nearby, a man fell backwards off the handrail and died shortly after impacting the pavement below. Even at our height many metres above the scene, we could see the significant damage to his skull and the ever-deepening pool of blood around his head. It was not the sort of spectacle we wanted to see, and the next morning's newspapers were a gruesome reminder of that fact. It was a tragic reminder that even when out having a good time, it was so important to be sensible – which sitting on a handrail that high above a road, was not.

Festuge started and finished in the space of just over a week, but Aarhus wasn't known affectionately as the party city for nothing. I had, by the time Festuge rolled around, become quite au fait with the Aarhus nightlife. Blitz was a multi-level nightclub, each level boasting its own unique features. It was always busy and its popularity could be attributed to its ability to deliver such a range of entertainment in the one venue. As popular as it was, I didn't visit that club very often. More frequent were my visits to Downtown, Lions and Sam's Bar. Downtown was a nightclub in the conventional sense but was rather expensive. It was with great appreciation therefore, that I accepted complimentary membership to the club and enjoyed all the corresponding benefits that such membership involved. Søren was the manager and had, some years earlier, backpacked around Australia and found the experience wonderful. He said that the Aussies had done so much for him on his travels, and he was only too keen to repay the hospitality. He couldn't do enough for me as he signed me up to membership and explained to me that I was always welcome in the club, as were any friends accompanying me. There would be no entrance fee for me, or my guests and I would enjoy a complimentary beverage on each visit. Consequently, there were some long nights spent at Downtown. Many of my classmates, who would have otherwise avoided Downtown, were grateful for my apparent networking abilities and, of course, entry at no charge.

Cafes and pubs were not unique to Aarhus as they could be found in numbers in any city countrywide. My favourite in Aarhus was Lions, slightly ahead of Cafe Jordan. It didn't take long before I was treated as a regular and on first name basis with all the staff. I was often treated to free pool in the downstairs entertainment rooms and even the occasional complimentary drink or two. I would take visiting exchange students there who would envy at the rapport I had with all the staff, most of whom would welcome me by name.

Sam's Bar was conceptually different from both the nightclubs and the cafes in Aarhus, but equally as enjoyable. Sam's Bar was a dedicated karaoke venue that was always busy and at which the patrons were the entertainment. For me, finding the right key meant rummaging in my pockets and I was, without doubt, tone deaf, but participation was always fun. I became well known at Sam's Bar, for perhaps more than anything else, my regular renditions of the Men at Work classic, *Down Under*. It was not because I sang so well, but because it was virtually all that I sang. There was method in my madness, though, as singing that song, albeit very poorly, would see me gain a lot of attention from so many other young people at the bar. It was, in many ways, an ice-breaker moment to the audience at large.

It seemed odd to me, but the development of my new language was also enhanced by my many visits to these nightspots. I found that when people were relaxed and enjoying themselves in often loud environments, the last thing they wanted to do was concentrate on a conversation in a language other than their own. Sure, in the early days, weeks and months, I would often be lost to such conversation, but necessity saw me learn quickly enough to correct that situation.

An abundant nightlife was certainly not the only attraction that drew thousands of visitors to Aarhus annually. Set just outside the heart of the city was Den Gamle By, which quite literally translated to The Old Town. I can't recall the number of visits I made to the quaint little village that so effortlessly provided the experience of Danish culture, dating back hundreds of years. There were over sixty old buildings dating back to as early as 1500 through to 1909 and included workshops, a chemist, a school and a post office. I visited Den Gamle By with school friends, with my host families and with many other exchange students visiting from other parts of Denmark. It gave an exceptional insight into the life of the city that I had quickly come to call my own and enabled a greater appreciation of the modern city that was Aarhus in 1992.

Tivoli Friheden was an amusement park that I would have liked to have visited more often. It was set in the background of an amazing flower display and boasted all the fun of the fair, concerts and restaurants. It was, in many ways, the smaller cousin to the world-famous Tivoli in Copenhagen, but still managed to deliver a thoroughly enjoyable experience on every visit.

A major attraction in Aarhus also happened to be one of its significant corporate citizens. In 1856, the Ceres Brewery began as a purely local enterprise and quickly developed into one of the country's most recognisable brands. Not only was it recognisable for its product, but also for the pungent odour that was obvious when walking past the brewery. Despite the odour, I visited the brewery several times throughout the year to participate in the tours that it offered. Ceres Brewery produced beer for every occasion – literally. It would release special ranges of beer at Easter and Christmas, all of which were usually far stronger than the ordinary brew. The release of special brew was not unique to Ceres, but perhaps was to Danish brewers generally.

On my first visit, I stood at the gates for about fifteen minutes waiting for Laerke and several of her friends to arrive. Laerke and I had met some weeks earlier on a night bus to Brabrand and having been rather intimate on that occasion, remained very good friends. At such close quarters, the powerful odour assaulted both my sense of smell and my sense of taste. I pondered the questions that I hoped would be answered by the tour, in particular, why such a smell was created in the process. When Laerke arrived with her friends, I discovered that of the eight of us, I was the only male. Of course, I had no complaints about that.

The tour started in a small but comfortable room, where we were shown a video about the history of the brewery and some of the most salient facts about its production rates, brands and consumer markets. At that stage of my exchange, much of the presentation was lost on me, given that it was presented in Danish. Apparently, they did have English versions of the video, and the guides could take the tours in English, but on each of my visits to the brewery, I was with Danish friends and therefore on each occasion the presentation was in Danish. Naturally, I understood far more of the tour on my visit later in the year.

From the small theatre room, we were escorted through a maze of old buildings that comprised the brewery. It was cold, but not frightfully so, and we were only outside for short periods as we went from one area of the brewery to another. The first of the production rooms was where they heated the malt and first filtered the beer. It was in this area that the concentration of the odour was most pronounced. Despite the smell, the room, and all the equipment, was impeccably clean, with the stainless-steel shining splendidly throughout. The second area was a great mass of stainless-steel pipes weaving their way up, down and around the walls and connecting with the large beer vats positioned around the room. It was explained that the yeast was added in that stage of the process. Once the beer was actually made, all that remained to be done was bottling, and that was the final area of the brewery to be explored. The fully automated process was impressive, as was the fact that it could bottle many thousands of beers per hour.

Our tour concluded with ninety minutes of beer tasting in the brewery's own bar. A quaint area with only about eight or nine tables, a charming little bar carved from solid timber and, of course, an abundance of Ceres beer. On each table there were laminated sheets of tasting notes for each of the beers as well as the history or inspiration behind them. Luckily, our table was positioned closest to the toilets! I had not intended the brewery tour to be an afternoon of excess, and even though I kept to drinking only one or two of each beer available, that was the result. Of course, when there were so many different types of beer to sample, just one or two of each amounted to a rather significant consumption.

As we were leaving the brewery, one of the waitresses slipped me a scribbled note containing her name and the message *Cafe Jordan – 19:30 xx*. Thankfully, she was discreet, as I was there with my close friend Laerke. I didn't even read it until after we had left the brewery and were walking to a cafe in town. Laerke and her friends left the cafe at around 6:00pm, but I said I was catching up with some classmates later. I went to Cafe Jordan and waited nervously until 7:30pm. I had no idea what to expect, or why Jannike gave me the note. It was apparent that not only was Jannike gorgeous, she was punctual to the minute. I stood to greet her and presented my hand. She grabbed it and pulled me toward her for a warm hug and quick kiss on the cheek. Naturally I was a bit shocked, but pleasantly so. She asked in Danish whether I spoke the language and with my embryonic vocabulary, I answered that I spoke a little. She reverted immediately to English and we proceeded to enjoy each other's company for another hour or so. I really was a little 'under the weather' and needed to go home. Jannike asked if we could meet again, to which I eagerly replied, "of course".

On the scribbled note, I added her telephone number and also gave her my host family's number in return.

One of my subsequent tours of the brewery was actually by Jannike's invitation. She was hosting several of her classmates from the Law Department at Aarhus University and asked me to join them. They had all recently finished a complicated law assignment and were out celebrating. That night, I ended up back at Jannike's place to spend what was left of the night with her in more intimate surroundings. I found it humorous that the brewery itself was named after the Roman fertility goddess 'Ceres', because Jannike was very much a goddess as far as I was concerned. However, I only saw Jannike once more, at which time she gave me a Ceres Brewery 'pin' for my Rotary jacket and several 'clean' beer bottle labels for my label collection.

It serves no useful purpose to list every attraction the city offered, save to say there were a great many. While I probably came close to doing so, I did not get to experience them all.

Based on my observations, Aarhus was a particularly cultural place. Its many museums, churches and galleries ensured that categorisation. My first taste of local culture was perhaps the concert I attended with Esben, the priest in my hosting Rotary Club. Upon honest reflection, I had initial misgivings about a rock concert the likes of which a priest would attend. Exchange had an uncanny knack of turning misgivings into good fortune, and I thoroughly enjoyed the concert and the company of Esben. It was held in Musikhuset (the concert hall) just adjacent to the Town Hall. The venue had beautifully landscaped grounds, with water features and pathways that were spectacular. The facade was made entirely of glass for the full length and height of the building, which added to the feeling of size throughout the foyer areas. It was open and airy and was a very popular destination for leading musical and theatrical acts to Aarhus. We were there to see Hanne Boel. Hanne was not only a talented musician but had a vast musical education. She had graduated from the Royal Danish Academy of Music, and also spent time at the much-famed Berklee School of Music in

Boston. Her several Grammy awards were no doubt testament to her talent, and I was most indebted to Esben for the wonderful experience of attending her concert. Once again, I had not been influenced by my misgivings, but instead by my desire to engage meaningfully with each and every opportunity presented to me by the Rotarians, who so kindly invited me to participate so often.

Aarhus also boasted the country's second largest university. It was an immaculate campus set around the University Park, which was comprised of a rolling landscape of lush grounds and feature ponds. The buildings were an intelligent mix of old and new with only minor modifications in style between the earliest buildings and the most current. When it commenced in 1928, the university only had 64 students, but by the time of my visit, the student population had multiplied to well over 20,000. It had graduated the heir to the Danish throne, Crown Prince Frederik, only a few years before my arrival. I was fortunate enough to develop an intimate knowledge of the university, both from an academic perspective, and socially. Given that my first host father was a Professor of History there and my first host brother, a student of Political Science, I became rather familiar with the campus. On several occasions I was guided around the university and was able to participate in parties there with my host brother and his classmates.

Aarhus was home to many foreigners who had immigrated to Denmark. It was, for 12 months, also home to this Australian, who by good luck or otherwise, found himself living as part of that wonderful city. I would like to think that a part of me remains with Aarhus and its people, because a great deal of Aarhus and its people remain with me.

11

Remembering Ry

Ry was such a small word but rather difficult to pronounce properly. It happened to be the name of the town in which two of my best exchange student friends lived. To some extent, it was fitting that the town had such a small name, as it was also a small Danish town. It was located just under forty kilometres west of Aarhus and took about forty minutes to travel there by train. With a population of only about 5,000 people, it was a close community. It sat in the heart of what was known as the Lake District and was surrounded by an interconnected system of lakes and watercourses. It was not surprising that with such an abundance of water, it was also the biggest forest district in Denmark and very popular for the Danes in summer.

The entire district was among the most historical in the country with stories of life dating back some 10,000 years. There was evidence of old Viking settlements and relics from the middle ages. It was truly a diverse area in that a tourist could visit one of Denmark's highest mountains, the grave of an abbot, or simply relax and camp by any number of spectacularly beautiful lakes all within a 15 to 20 kilometre radius.

Despite all my trips to Ry, I only enjoyed a small number of the attractions the region had to offer. Ry for me, was far more than simply a beautiful haven for relaxation. I relaxed very little during my visits.

It was also where Matthew was hosted for the duration of his exchange and, as such, was a place I frequented. Each visit would involve spending at least one night, often more and there were at least ten such visits throughout my twelve months of exchange.

Matthew, Michael and I would often visit each other's school and in doing so, broadened our circles of Danish friends significantly. This was the case at Matthew's school, which was in a nearby town called Silkeborg. That town was considerably larger than Ry and in addition to visiting for school, we would often enjoy the nightlife that Silkeborg had to offer. As a result of my frequent visits to Matthew's school, I befriended an adorable girl named Mille. I had never met a sweeter, more caring girl in my life and seriously doubted whether I ever would. Our first night out was to a local nightclub called Avalon, and two or three other bars and cafes. After the last bar closed, we walked back to Mille's house. As we passed the local bakery, the smell of freshly baked bread lured us to the rear of the shop. There we were able to buy some bread rolls that were so fresh, they were still warm from the oven. The three of us simply sat on Mille's bed, enjoying the bread rolls and each other's company, until the morning sun suggested that Matthew and I should return to his host family's house. Matthew and I would often spend nights at Mille's place watching videos and listening to music. My old videos of the Miami High's *Rock and Roll Eisteddfods* were popular, as were my photographs from home. As our friendship developed, it transpired that several of my visits to Ry saw me stay not at Matthew's house, but with Mille. On one terrific night late in the year, my relationship with Mille went well beyond that of friends.

Mille was hosting a party for a large number of her friends and, thankfully, I had long been included in that demographic. We ate enormous amounts of pizza and barbecued chicken, washed down, of course, by copious amounts of alcohol. That combination was satisfying, but not nearly as satisfying as the events that transpired throughout the evening. Once the party had slowed a little, there were only about eight of us left and we were all in Mille's room. We discussed everything from music, movies, likes and dislikes, dares and other mischief we had all been up to in the past. I ended up jumping out of Mille's bedroom window, even though it was on the first floor of her house. The garden made for a soft landing and, from there, I ran down her backyard, along the jetty and jumped into the freezing cold lake. I was oblivious to the stupidity of it all as I executed the dare without fear. It seemed, though, that the stupidity was contagious, as most of the others soon joined me jumping in and out of the freezing lake. The others simply dried off, but Mille invited me to shower with her and I just couldn't resist. I had imagined her without clothes many times before, but seeing her naked far exceeded even that which I had imagined. We showered until the hot water ran out and returned to her bedroom to re-join the remaining few. Over the weeks that followed, Mille also visited me in Aarhus and we wrote dozens of letters to each other. Mille, who was particularly gifted creatively, also wrote me poems that I knew would be cherished forever. The letters were almost like contracts in which we confirmed our feelings for each other.

We'd fallen deeply in love, but somehow remained well aware of the fact that I would, in only a few months' time, be leaving Denmark for good. It was important for both of us to ensure that we were going to be able to deal with that inevitability. We decided that love had, and then lost, was better than not having experienced it at all and continued to let ours flourish. In a testament to our love, I was nervous about whether I had the strength to deal with the necessary end to that relationship.

As was commonplace for many exchange students, I was encouraged by the fact that I had already engaged in that emotional struggle a few times. Ironically, Ry was the setting for one such earlier battle with my emotions.

Nicole, from Canada, was also hosted in Ry and had, earlier in the year, enjoyed several visits from me. We had cemented what was unquestionably our love during the Euro-Tour and this continued during my visits with her in Ry. So serious were we, that we had discussed plans for her to move to Australia after my return in January 1993 and what opportunities there would be for her at university and work. The word marriage was mentioned by us more than once.

I even met her mother and aunt when they visited from Canada and that was on the basis of me being Nicole's love. It was Sunday, 14 June 1992 and the only time my visit to Ry did not involve spending the night – we just didn't have the time. In the company of her mother and aunt, we visited a nearby Catholic Monastery, which had been abandoned many years prior. It had been converted to a museum and served as a reminder of earlier times. It was all interesting, but without doubt, the most interesting was a room full of human skulls showing evidence of a primitive form of brain surgery! We returned to a cafe to share lunch and enjoy each other's company for the last time. There was truly something special between Nicole and me. We had experienced many of the wonders of Europe together and had enjoyed some very private and intimate moments. I had not, at that time, ever felt such sadness at saying goodbye. Nicole was leaving Denmark early the next morning and travelling with her mother and aunt to various European destinations. After that, they were flying back to Canada. I stood on the platform and hugged Nicole for what seemed like an eternity, interrupted only by the arrival of my train. We exchanged vows to visit each other, either in Australia or Canada, but I feared deep down, that we both knew the promises were a naive attempt to ease the pain. I boarded my train and took a seat by the window. Nicole was in the comforting embrace of her mother looking at me through eyes filled with tears. I remained composed, but only until my train pulled from the station. I realised that while my departure from Denmark was still some 6 months away, it showed me how difficult it was going to be to leave, and I didn't like it at all. For perhaps the first time on exchange, I feared my own return to Australia.

It was almost a prerequisite to any romance on exchange, that both would acknowledge the harsh reality that the duration of it was, unavoidably, limited. It was a conscious choice to accept the quality of an experience, rather than the quantity of it and focus always on the positive times. There were plenty of those with Nicole in Ry, even in the weeks leading up to her departure.

I had spent three days staying with Nicole and her host family earlier that month. That time was simply spent together – sharing photographs from the recent Euro-Tour, watching videos from home and enjoying what was a protracted period of wonderful weather. On one of the days, we enjoyed a unique adventure together. A friend of Nicole's host father owned an American style 'ranch' and had several horses. Knud was entirely generous and let us take two of the most magnificent horses I had ever seen for a long ride. I was given a horse named Royal Rembrandt and as far as horses go, he indeed appeared 'royal'. He was an imposing beast, standing some seventeen hands in the equine measure. His beautiful coat was a clean and smooth light-brown colour, and he appeared to have black socks just above his hooves on all but one leg. It was just his colouring. I didn't know that much about horses, but Knud was extremely passionate about them – especially those in his own stable. He spent quite some time that morning telling us about the horses, where we could ride and what to expect. Royal Rembrandt was a Danish Warmblood and although spirited, was suitable for a novice rider. Nicole's horse was named Dream Diva and was a beautiful chocolate colour with light patches predominantly positioned along her hind quarter. Knud told us that the pattern of colouring was a common attribute among Appaloosa horses and that she was a fine example of that breed. He also told us that if we got lost, she would find her own way back. I was a little nervous about riding Royal Rembrandt as I hadn't ridden a horse in a very long time. My fears were quickly dispelled after only moments on him.

Nicole and I each had backpacks on, filled with a picnic lunch, some red wine and a blanket. It was the type of adventure dreams are made of and on which love stories are based. We rode peacefully through some of the most picturesque countryside, down to one of the many lakes in the district. The wildflowers were in full bloom, the sky was a brilliant clear blue, the weather was warm and the water was crystal clear. It was as though we were the only people on an untouched, perfect earth. As we sat on the shore of the lake, sipping wine and enjoying our open rye bread sandwiches, we contemplated just how special the moment was and just how special youth exchange was in our lives. Although we knew that we were not the only people on earth, we were confident that we were the only people within many kilometres of our lakeside location. Safe in the knowledge that the horses wouldn't tell our secrets, we abandoned our clothes, took a swim in the lake and enjoyed more of the intimate moments that had become so much a part of our relationship. Time was once more the enemy and before we knew it, we had been gone a little over four hours. We were about half an hour away from the stables, so decided to take the most direct path home. Once at the stables, we both helped Knud unsaddle the horses and brush them down – it was an absolute pleasure to do so after the part they played in our extraordinary day.

Only days later, Nicole joined with me to help Matthew celebrate his 18th birthday. My 18th birthday had been spent with my host family in Odense and had been a very low-key affair. Matthew's, on the other hand, was a most boisterous event as his party was held jointly with two of his schoolmates who were also turning 18. A community hall had been booked and there were around 150 people running around in fewer and fewer clothes as the evening charged on. It was summer, so the midnight swim in a nearby lake wasn't too bad. Actually, it was a timely tonic against the ill effects of the alcohol consumed all night. Returning to the hall, I curled up on the stage and managed a few hours of sleep. Around 8:00am, the band started playing again, which, given I had curled up just near the drum kit, ended my painfully short sleep.

Ry occupied only a small part of the land, but I knew it would always represent a large part of my memories of Denmark. I was richer for having had so many wonderful experiences in and around that town, made that way by so many fantastic people.

12

Family Three

Aage and Agnes were my final host parents and lived in the same suburb as Carl and Marie. Aage was not a tall man, but had a larger-than-life personality evidenced in part by a life-sized cardboard effigy of himself in the bar room of their home. He liked to keep active and would regularly take walks in the nearby Marselisborg forest and would, each year, participate with his sons in the Aarhus marathon. Agnes was actually English born, although having lived in Denmark for decades, was very much a local. Agnes was a very sensitive lady who was abundantly gifted in her artistic and craft pursuits. As with my families before them, Aage and Agnes had a family pet. Like Vanja at Bendt and Clara's place, Scarlett was a German Shepherd. Unlike Vanja, Scarlett was much older and far less active. Despite her age, she enjoyed walks with the family in the nearby forest. Aage and Agnes had previously hosted exchange students, including one from my hometown.

Their home was both historic and very comfortable indeed. The house was built in the 1800s and, at one time in its long history, was home to the head of the Danish underground during the war. In fact, during some renovations many years prior to my exchange, a secret dungeon was discovered. It contained remnants from the underground movement, some old weaponry and maps. Most interestingly, there had been an elaborate series of tunnels connecting the house to the surrounding areas. They were closed off, as was the dungeon and, with that, a final closing of that chapter in the life of the house. Comprised of three levels and a detached three-car garage, there was ample room for guests. It had, on its basement level, a guest room, my bedroom and bathroom, a bar room complete with beer on tap, dart board and snooker table, a cellar well stocked with fine wine and a large laundry. One could get lonely in such a home, if it were not for such a large family. Aage and Agnes had four children, although only two of the boys resided at home. Frede was a few years older than me and lived at home with his girlfriend. He, much like Erik at the start of my exchange, very quickly became my 'big brother'. Victor was exactly my age and had in the same year, returned from his Rotary Youth Exchange in Australia. He was hosted in Victoria and had thoroughly enjoyed his time 'Down Under'. Aage and Agnes had also taken the opportunity to visit Victor in Australia, so they were familiar with many aspects of my homeland. It was great to have so many things in common with Victor, and we rapidly discovered that those commonalities extended beyond our age, our both being exchange students and his time in my home country.

An exchange student will experience a change in family values, morals and rules with each host family. This was consistent with a change in the personalities of the host parents. What is also different, in most instances, is the vocational background of the host parents. In the case of Agnes, however, she was primarily concerned with running the household, as was Marie in my second host family. Aage was the director of one of Scandinavia's largest advertising companies and was following in his father's footsteps in doing so. He was serious about his work and committed to the growth of his business. At the same time, however, he always found time for a life outside of the office with his family.

I had, before my scheduled change to this family, spent time with them in the summer. It was yet another of the many encroachments on my time with Carl and Marie, that had so characterised my summer months in Denmark. On 16 July 1992, Aage and Agnes took my host brother Victor and me to Spain. Aage's family owned an amazing hillside retreat on the hills that rose steeply from the shores of the Mediterranean in the north of Spain. The house was in a small Spanish town called Roses, which was in the province of Girona, about an hour's drive north of Barcelona. It was a beautiful town, with large palm trees lining Avinguda de Rhode, which was the road that ran parallel to the very wide beach along the length of Roses. There were a multitude of beaches and coves along the coast with steep rocky cliffs overlooking them. The summer house sat on one of those rocky hills almost immediately above The Port of Roses. The port was home to hundreds of fishing trawlers and other vessels, as well as fresh seafood markets when the trawlers returned with their catch.

For such a beautiful town, it had endured a devastating history. As early as the first decades of the 16th Century, Roses was attacked by forces from North Africa. As a result, fortifications were built to protect the town from such attack. However, before they were completed in 1553, the Turkish navy plundered the town, resulting in further additions to the fortification. Part of that additional security was the Castell de la Trinitat. The ruin of the castle still existed and, as it turned out, was located within a short walk of the summer house. In its day, several soldiers would reside at the fort at any given time, and it housed a reasonable armoury. It sat about sixty metres above sea level and was built over three levels. The highest point was further up the hill with the lower levels facing toward the Mediterranean. Despite the further fortification, Roses still fell in 1645 during the Catalan Revolt, again in 1712 during the War of the Spanish Succession and, after a relatively long period of calm, fell once more in the Wars of the French Revolution. There were some smaller skirmishes throughout its tortured history, but ultimately from the early 1800s, it remained very much Spanish.

The town also boasted one of the world's best restaurants. It won its first 'Michelin Star' in 1976 and its second only two years before I visited. It was opened in 1964 and was named elBulli after the owner's French bulldogs. I was told that the restaurant was actually ranked in the top fifty restaurants world-wide.

The summer house itself was typically Spanish with its red terracotta tiling and white rendered exterior. The rooftop was flat, allowing for rooftop entertaining and splendid panoramic views to the ocean and village below. Typical of the immediate area, but not necessarily of Spanish design generally, this house was huge. It had two kitchens, three bathrooms, two lounge rooms and four double bedrooms. I was spoiled, with a larger-than-normal double bed, my own balcony and a share of the stunning views. Given that the house was built on the side of this hill, the pool was accessed from the rooftop level. We were blessed with fine hot weather every day and made full use of the pool. The Mediterranean was so clear, so blue and so inviting, that it was often preferred to the pool. We were truly spoiled, because we would get hot and sweaty in our walk down to the ocean to then enjoy its cooling waters. After walking back up the steep road from the ocean or the town, we would again cool off in the soothing waters of the pool.

I was certainly exposed to many aspects of the Spanish culture during my stay in Roses. The tradition of siesta was observed with virtually all the traders closing for a couple of hours in the middle of the day. I was never one for sleep during the day, so I would spend the time exploring the town, the nearby coves or snorkelling along the large piers around the Port. Once or twice, I did use the siesta time to simply sit on the rooftop deck and read. Having enjoyed some hearty lunches in the summer heat at Roses, I could well understand why people would take a nap to defeat the post-lunch lethargy, but I just couldn't bring myself to actually go to sleep. I wanted to use every waking moment to savour the sights and sounds of my very different surroundings. My host family also enjoyed eating and drinking typically Spanish cuisine and beverage, which I also came to appreciate.

Perhaps the cultural highlight for me was attending a bullfight held at Plaza de Toros in the nearby provincial capital, Girona. Plaza de Toros was an historic bullfighting arena, built in 1897 and had a seating capacity of around eight thousand. In addition to bullfights, the arena would play host to other entertainment, such as the occasional visiting circus. Girona was only about half an hour away from Roses by bus, the ticket for which was included when we purchased the tickets to the bullfights. Aage and Agnes were not interested in attending the bullfights, although they were more than happy to allow Victor and I to do so.

Had I not experienced the bullfights for myself, I would have remained ignorant as to the process. The fact that there was a distinction between the role of the picador, the banderillero and the matador would have remained a mystery to me. The very existence of performers other than the matador was enlightening. Observation, coupled with a program containing poorly translated passages in English, taught me that the picador was the first 'fighter' to engage with the bull. His role was to pierce the muscle group on the back of the bull's neck with a sharp lance called a pica. Unlike those after him, he would do this from horseback. It was designed to fatigue the bull and, if successful, cause the bull to lower its head and further expose its shoulders. Next was the banderillero, who would spear colourful sticks with barbed points into the top of the bull's shoulder. These 'sticks' were called banderillas, hence the name of the fighter. These would often remain in the bull's shoulder for the remainder of the fight and further fatigue the bull. Finally, once the bull had been fought by the picador and banderillero, the matador would enter the ring. He would attempt to exhaust the bull even further, by having it charge at his cape, before inflicting the final blow. A large sword would then be thrust into the shoulders, piercing the aorta.

The event on the day of our visit began with a parade of the bullfighters competing that day, together with some elaborately decorated floats. The matadors included Curro Molina and Julio Campano, who were said to be very accomplished bullfighters. The matadors, dressed quite exquisitely in black and white, red and gold and also white and gold, were not nearly as big as I thought they would be. There were some short speeches, all of which were exclusively in Spanish and thus useless to me. Then there was the sounding of a trumpet, which apparently signalled the commencement of the fight. Most of the bullfights that day lasted between 80 -100 minutes, but I wasn't really keeping time. Following the final bullfight, I made my way to one of a number of bloodstained rooms under the arena, where the defeated bulls were butchered. The butchers, hard at work, were completely saturated in the warm blood of the brave bulls. It was not really my purpose to pass judgement on the merits of such actions, more to observe and to learn – even if it meant being splattered with a few drops of blood. While watching one of the bulls being butchered, I saw the lady who had been responsible for presenting the ear of the bull to the bullfighters in recognition of a first-class fight. We had obvious and insurmountable language difficulties, yet I was able to convince her to allow me the privilege of a photograph with her. She was blessed with amazing beauty and appeared gentle despite the somewhat gruesome role she played in the bullfights suggesting otherwise.

I departed Plaza de Toros and Girona that day with very mixed feelings. I had experienced a spectacle that was an integral part of Spanish culture and one that attracted an audience in the tens of millions every year. It was obvious that the traditions of bullfighting dated back hundreds of years and had, over that time, developed a most glorified public image. I learned that the leading matadors could earn many thousands of dollars per fight. Without exception, I always looked to respect the culture and traditions of the places I visited throughout Europe. I always looked upon culture as something that enhanced or enriched people or society, something that had certain defining qualities. As I pondered these thoughts, I couldn't reconcile such notions of culture with what I saw as, really, a vicious and cruel spectacle. There was certainly much pomp and ceremony about the 'performance' aspects of the bullfight – the colours, the sounds, the costumes, the screaming of olé and the long history. But the justification of such an event on cultural grounds seemed lacking to me. It occurred to me that what I had just witnessed was one of the extremely few things in Europe that I had no desire to ever see again. I was grateful for having experienced it and held no regret, but could not justify contributing to the future torture of these animals by the payment of admission. Such was the impact of these thoughts that I found myself writing about them in my diary, in letters home to family and friends, and discussing them with Aage, Agnes and Victor upon our return to Roses. The extent of this internal and external dialogue simply confirmed for me that the memory was indelible.

There was another sporting spectacle taking place during my stay in Spain and I was fortunate enough to experience the atmosphere of it at close quarters. Bullfighting was considered a sport by the Spanish, however, there was no comparison with the event that was taking place only an hour's drive south of Roses. The 1992 Olympic Games were being hosted by Barcelona, and the city was alive with visitors from nations the world over. While I didn't have tickets to any of the ceremonies or events, I was able to savour the atmosphere that was ever-present in and around Barcelona. On a cruise around the harbour, we saw many of the opening ceremony sets stored on trailers and in warehouses. I was able to photograph one of the main opening ceremony pieces – a large parade float piece designed in the shape of a gigantic birthday cake and adorned with the Olympic Rings and other decorations unique to the 1992 Games. A particularly special moment for me happened as we dined at a cafe in the heart of Barcelona. We were all enjoying the refreshment that only a cold ale can provide on a very hot day, when a number of Australian athletes walked by in team Australia colours. They were part of the national field hockey team known as the Kookaburras and I was suitably proud and moved to be able to wish them my best as they prepared for the days ahead. I was later delighted to read that they won the silver medal.

Barcelona was, of course, very much more than simply the Olympic City. It was, in its own right, a most wonderful place to visit. It was rather densely populated, which was not surprising given that there were only about five or so kilometres between the shores of the Mediterranean and the mountainous range of Collserola to the west. A significant part of those ranges was declared a metropolitan park, which was more than twenty times larger than Central Park in New York. The diversity of forests, waterways, scrublands and Savannah grasslands resulted in an equally diverse range of animals living in the park, from rabbits, squirrels and badgers, to eagles, giant turtles and lizards. What was particularly interesting was the Torre de Collserola – a telecommunications tower that stood almost 300 metres high on one of the ridges of the range. The tower was visible from most parts of Barcelona and in turn, certainly provided a spectacular view over the city. The architecture was quite fascinating as the tower was effectively held in place by many steel cables anchored to the ground. The tower was built specifically for the Olympics, or more accurately, to address the increased telecommunications needs of the city because of the Olympics. So new was the tower that the public viewing platform had not been opened to the public at the time of my visit.

We were able to take in some extraordinary sights, of which Barcelona really does have an embarrassment of riches. The Santa Maria del Mar was a stunning basilica in the Catalan-Gothic style. It was intriguing to read that the basilica had been built very quickly with construction taking just fifty-five years. I figured that 'quickly' in that sense was a comparative term given that it was completed in 1384. In that time and compared to other significant construction of that era, fifty-five years probably was 'quick'. It boasted impressive square buttresses, flat-topped octagonal towers and plain surfaces – which of itself was a defining characteristic.

Perhaps one of the most famous sights in Barcelona was the Columbus Monument. Standing some sixty metres tall, the monument to renowned explorer Christopher Columbus was as impressive as his discoveries. The large bronze statue of Columbus atop the Corinthian column was an immediately recognisable feature of the monument, but closer observation revealed a great deal more detail. The pedestal upon which the column stood, was adorned with four bronze statues of winged females, each representing the four-corners of the world. Below that, was the massive octagonal plinth upon which the rest of the monument stood. The plinth was inset with eight bronze panels that represented aspects of Columbus' first voyage to the Americas. I didn't spend a great deal of time examining them all but was able to ascertain that they included a scene where Columbus and his son were asking for food at a monastery and where, on his return to Barcelona, he met with the King and Queen.

By the time of our visit to Barcelona, I had lost count of the number of breathtaking churches and cathedrals I had seen throughout Europe. While many of the striking features of those churches and cathedrals were shared, virtually every one of them boasted something unique; something that distinguished them as being very different from the others. I certainly never tired of visiting them. It never ceased to amaze me how basically a mass of bricks, stone, mortar, marble, granite, timber, bronze, brass and glass could be so moving. I was always left in awe at the endeavour of those responsible for the design and construction of such buildings. This was certainly true of my visit to the Sagrada Familia Basilica. I simply stood and stared at the façade of the church as we approached. I photographed it, then photographed it again. Had it not been for the fact I used my film sparingly, I would have photographed it many more times. I could not recall immediately whether any other church or cathedral had so overwhelmed me. Sure, the Strasbourg Cathedral de Notre Dame certainly struck an imposing figure across the Strasbourg skyline, and to the discerning visitor, was a source of much admiration. Similarly, there was the ever-famous

Cathedral Notre Dame in Paris, but even that shared the Paris skyline with equally or more famous structures. I found it astonishing that the construction of the church was still being undertaken 110 years after it had begun and because it was an expiatory church, donations alone had financed the building. This funding was interrupted during the Spanish Civil War and, in later years, proceeds of ticket sales helped continue the building.

Throughout the streets of Barcelona, we were approached several times by people purporting to sell tickets to the Opening Ceremony. The dubious nature of some of these people, coupled with the fact they were asking exorbitant amounts for the tickets, ensured that we would be watching the Opening Ceremony on television from the comfort of our holiday house. I was always intensely patriotic, which made the experience of cheering for two countries, Australia and Denmark, all the more unusual. In many ways, having two countries to cheer for enhanced my experience of the Olympics. My new-found loyalty to Denmark came to an abrupt halt, however, when Australia played Denmark in football. The Danes in the house heavily outnumbered me, but I stood firm in my support of the Aussies. My unfailing support of the Australians was rewarded with a 3 – 0 win, much to my pleasure. Aage's brother-in-law George, was also visiting the house from England and, following my win in the football, was tempted to place a bet with me that Australia would not win a single gold medal. I was not a betting man, particularly when I was on an exchange student's budget, but chose to accept the bet. In preparing for my exchange, I researched many facts and figures about Australia. Fortuitously for me, one such fact was that Australia was one of only five countries to have competed at every modern Olympic Games and since my birth, had averaged more than ten medals in each Olympics. At least a couple of those medals had been gold, so I was supremely confident of winning and win I did. I won 100 English Pounds which came in very useful upon my return to Aarhus. I suspected that the bet was made as a way to simply gift some money to me. It would have otherwise been quite absurd for him to make such a bet. George was rather wealthy and was actually the great grandson of David Livingstone. When I was first told that he was related to David Livingstone, I was only vaguely familiar with the name. It wasn't until I returned to Denmark that I researched him and reminded myself that Livingstone was a doctor, missionary and explorer who was famous for trying to introduce Christianity and commerce to Africa in the 1800s. George had brought his new Jaguar to Spain with him and on more than one occasion offered to let me drive it. Of course, I declined, both because it was against the Rotary rules, and because I didn't want to risk damaging such a luxury vehicle.

Another event that will long remain cherished in my memory was, quite simply one of our nightly dinners. We were dining at home and were entertaining a number of guests. One of Aage's aunts was married to a Frenchman and had lived in the south of France for some thirty years. They were both visiting the house. Aage's sister and George were also visiting and on that particular night, a Spanish friend of the family who looked after the house year round was also dining with us. My presence made it five different nationalities sitting around the one dinner table. The accepted language over dinner had to be English as that was the language most common to us all. That night's feast was beyond description, but more enjoyable still was the interaction of all those present.

Fishing was one of the prime industries in Roses, and each weekday morning we were able to observe a tradition among the fishermen. At approximately 6:45am, more than twenty large fishing boats would line up in the harbour and wait for a loud siren to sound at exactly 7:00am. No boat was permitted to leave for the day until after the sounding of this siren. They would return late in the evening and unload their respective catches for the seafood markets the next morning. The markets themselves were a sight to behold, even though the pungent stench was something most would rather avoid. While certainly not as sophisticated as the stock exchange or many other industrialised markets around the world, the manner in which local traders went about purchasing product was an interesting observation of local behavioural norms. Individuals too, could buy directly from the markets, which we did on several mornings. The quality of the seafood was simply sensational.

The real attraction of the holiday was that there was more than enough time to do everything or to do nothing. Many days were spent simply lazing by the pool or on the beach below. There were, of course, many other days spent experiencing wonderful adventures in and around Roses and the northern extremities of Spain. On one such venture out, we drove to the site at which the Olympic Torch had arrived in Spain and had begun its journey to Barcelona. An impressive monument had been constructed in honour of that event. Nearby, was an amazing archaeological site featuring such artefacts as a Greek water filter from around the Third Century BC. It was made from ceramic pipes, which were positioned in such a way that water would have to pass through several pipes before being used. The remnants of old stone housing were remarkably well preserved which made the study of them so much more accurate. I was fortunate enough to have observed a number of archaeologists at work on the site and even more fortunate still, to have been given the opportunity to speak with them over lunch. It gave me such a sense of satisfaction and achievement to be able to write to the History Department at my former high school and inform them of such an adventure. The profound privilege was not lost on me, that over the course of my travels through Europe, I had been given the opportunity to see or experience aspects of history studied at home – this archeological dig was yet another such example.

On our penultimate night in Roses, Victor and I decided to return to an exciting nightclub we had visited earlier in our stay. Hollywoods played fantastic music, was aesthetically pleasing, and on that night, was extremely well attended. It was very different to the club of the same name that Matthew and I visited when in London. Perhaps part of the reason I found the music so enjoyable was that much of it was rock and roll – from the sixties, seventies and eighties. I had enjoyed several different types of local beer during our stay in Roses and even learned a little about them. Estrella Damm, for example, was a brewery founded by August Kuentzmann Damm in 1872. August and his wife fled the Alsace region of France during the Franco-Prussian War and found their way to Barcelona. Over one hundred years later, the brewery was still owned by the descendants of August Damm and produced some of the region's most popular beer. With a flavour as imposing as its history, Estrella Damm was my chosen beer for the entire night. The potent mix of Estrella Damm, great music, the company of my host brother and simply the joy of being in Spain resulted in the abandonment of all inhibitions. In that mindset, I felt entirely comfortable approaching a young woman who was dancing alone. Her name was Bonita and she was exceptionally attractive. I wasn't sure if she was being truthful or not when she told me that her Spanish name meant 'pretty', but I was certain that it would be appropriate if indeed, it did. She had the darkest brown eyes I had ever seen, and I certainly looked into them from close quarters. Her voice was sweet, but husky and was spoken through the softest red lips I could remember. Her smooth skin was a dark olive colour and having danced for some time, glistened with a light sweat. Her command of English was reasonable but rarely used while we danced. It was too loud to properly talk on the dance floor and given that her dancing was very spirited, I was without sufficient breath to talk much anyway. At almost 4:00am, Victor and I decided it was time to return home. Bonita put her arms around me and whispered in my ear. She said that good times never end if you have something to remind you of them and with that, started kissing me. After what felt like several minutes, I had serious reservations about returning home. Of course, it would not have been appropriate to stay, so Victor and I returned to the house and enjoyed a quick swim before finally getting to bed at about 4:30am.

Our final day in Roses was one of complete relaxation. Aage had to have a sleep, because we were going to commence our two-thousand-kilometre drive back to Aarhus later that afternoon. I wanted to enjoy the last of the glorious Spanish weather and spent most of the day swimming in the Mediterranean Sea. At one stage, I simply floated on my back and reflected on how supremely fortunate I had been to have just experienced over two weeks in Spain. I had tasted new food, met new people, observed and participated in new culture and seen some amazing sights. I felt immersed, not in the Mediterranean, but in a sea of gratitude.

Life at Aage and Agnes's house was, for me, a further example of my great fortune on exchange. As with all my families, I truly felt like I belonged – that I was a part of the family. I had much in common with my host brother Victor, most notably Rotary Youth Exchange. More importantly though, we were both the same age and were able to enjoy many nights in the city together, playing pool and meeting new friends. As had happened so many times on exchange, a strong bond developed between the two of us. So, too, with my other host brothers and sister in that family, but perhaps to a lesser extent.

Living with Aage and Agnes could be distinguished from living with my other host families. Certainly, their home was considerably larger as it really needed to be given that the family itself was considerably larger in number. But the true distinction arose from fact that living with them involved an exploration of endings. I was living with my last host family, playing with my last host pet and residing in the last Danish home. It was in the company of this very special group of people that I enjoyed the last months of my youth exchange. Despite the multitude of emotions as the end drew near, I was able to recognise even then, that it was the family's understanding, unconditional support and love, that helped make those often trying times, much less difficult.

13

Christmas Traditions

Christmas was always a special time of the year, although inevitably for exchange students, it was extra special. Quite apart from being thousands of kilometres away from their families, exchange students from Australia were, more often than not, in vastly different climates and cultures. Fortunately for me, I was able to experience the weather that was traditionally associated with Christmas. White fluffy snow and temperatures below zero were simply never experienced on the Gold Coast, especially at Christmas time. Additionally, the culture in Denmark at Christmas was vastly different. Perhaps the most striking cultural difference was the fact that the Danes celebrated more on Christmas Eve than they did on Christmas Day. These Christmas Eve celebrations varied from family to family, but usually involved an abundance of delicious food, plenty of fine beverage and ingredients common the world over – love, happiness and good cheer.

The Christmas season, however, also marked the nearing of the end for me as an exchange student in Denmark. I had stayed in touch with my temporary host family in Odense, although I had not been able to return. I was determined to see them one last time that year, so I made the necessary arrangements to visit them for a few days. I was delighted to discover that they were as excited about my return as I was. On Friday, 4 December 1992, I boarded the train and headed for

Odense. There was a distinct difference in my return trip when compared to my first train travel from Odense to Aarhus. I knew where I was going, with whom I was to meet and had a far greater command of the language than I did in the preceding January. As the train ground to a slow squeaky halt, memories of my early days in Odense overwhelmed me. I found that I was unable to rise from my seat and instead allowed a solitary tear to well in my eye. It was the realisation that I had started my exchange with this family and was returning to bid them farewell after an amazing year. The train wasn't terminating at Odense, so I couldn't allow myself to wallow in thought for very long. Just as I left the train, so too did the tear from my eye. With a heavy heart, but a most positive outlook, I collected my luggage and made my way to the platform.

Josefine, too, had returned to Odense for Christmas with her family and was there to escort me back to Stockfletsvej one last time. I remembered being awestruck at her beauty the first time we had met and that sensation wasn't lost all those months later. Josefine was intensely attractive and reminding myself that she was my host sister was often difficult to do. We returned home to a full house with all the family home for the Christmas period. Astrid, Freja and Ida had toiled in the kitchen, so when we arrived, lunch was already laid out waiting for us. I was always well fed in Denmark, evidenced perhaps by my growing waistline. It was certainly nothing I ever complained about, as quite frankly, I enjoyed it too much. It wasn't until after 2:00am the next morning that I finally made my way to bed. Several hours were spent simply recounting adventures from throughout my year and showing photographs I had taken. Considerable time had been spent talking in such a manner with my entire host family, but the later few hours were spent privately with Josefine. The enticing aroma of breakfast lured me upstairs later that morning, despite being rather tired. This was not at all unlike my first morning in Denmark many months earlier.

I rode my host father's bicycle into town to simply remember and cherish the places that were my first taste of Danish society. Again, the places had not changed, but my ability to read signs and converse with the people most certainly had. I visited a large shopping centre with some 90 specialty stores, one of which employed Josefine on a casual basis. I could have easily sat and talked with Josefine for several hours, but knew she had to work. Riding onto the campus at which my Danish language first started to develop was very surreal. Some eleven months earlier, I had arrived at the school with my Danish vocabulary limited to not much more than four or five words and struggled daily with learning the language. There I was those eleven months later with a command of the language that enabled me to understand every aspect of those earlier teachings and to answer any of the questions that had been posed during those weeks. Fundamentally, I had 'become Danish' to such a degree that nothing seemed foreign to me as it had when my exchange first started.

Later that evening, Josefine and I ventured into town. We played pool, enjoyed some drinks and danced until the nightclubs closed. Once home, we again found ourselves in Josefine's room talking and listening to music. It was the music of our hearts that played the loudest and only added to the feelings that had existed from the earliest of days. Josefine's singing was all consuming, and her voice would make angels envious. Normally Josefine would reserve her talent for the Danish girls' choir, but made an exception for me. As the two of us shared solitude before the piano, she played and sang *Right Here Waiting* by Richard Marx. As she sang the lyrics, *I took for granted, all the times that I thought would last somehow*, I broke down. It was not that I had taken my time in Odense for granted, in reality, the opposite was true. Indeed, not a moment of my entire exchange was taken for granted – it was far too precious. However, I knew that my time in Odense would not last and was rather limited. As early as our briefing camps, I was fully informed about the fleeting nature of the exchange experience. Despite this, the lyrics really brought to the foremost of my mind, that not only was my time in Odense limited, my exchange year was quickly approaching its end. I was not ordinarily emotional, but in those circumstances, I was openly so and felt not even the slightest compulsion to try and subdue the feelings. I fell asleep, content in the honesty between us, but saddened by the knowledge I would soon be 'oceans apart' from the incredible people of Denmark.

The next morning, I had to be woken, which was unusual for me. After breakfast, we all spent the morning tending to chores in the garden. The flagpole was taken down for cleaning, leaves were raked and garden soil turned. It was quite cold, but the activity warmed us all. Our appetites were satisfied by a delicious lunch, before Josefine and I joined some of her friends in town for ice skating. It was only my second time ice skating, but I was able to enjoy the experience tremendously. Part of the enjoyment was not actually in the ice skating, but in an awkward moment for Josefine and one of her friends. Christina arrived a little late, she arrived just as we had finished lacing our skates. As she hurriedly sat down beside us, she said to Josefine, "so this is the man you've been so excited about." Of course, Christina didn't realise I could understand every word and we all blushed and shared a slightly embarrassed laugh. As a family, we had another late night simply sipping coffee and sharing stories. There was so much to talk about, it felt so right to do so, but the disappearing hours were relentless.

The next day was that which I dreaded most. It was the day I had to bid my host family farewell for the final time. I was nonetheless heartened by the fact that it was a busy day, including a visit with the Rotary Club that had temporarily hosted me during the Odense language course. I was remembered by some but welcomed by all. I discovered repeatedly during my exchange, that fate always had its part to play. I missed the train I was scheduled to take back to Aarhus, but this turned out to be fortuitous. Had I caught the earlier train, I would not have met Carsten again. Carsten, also known by those on the Euro-

Tour as 'King Bart', had also been visiting in Odense and had a train to catch that afternoon. It was Carsten who noticed me, although that wasn't at all surprising given I was wearing my Rotary exchange jacket. We were not catching the same train, which was a shame as we were not able to share memories for long. There was enough time though, to introduce him to my amazing Odense family and to recount how wonderful it had been living as a part of that family, albeit for a short while. It was also an opportunity to further demonstrate the continued development of my Danish language to Carsten. The last time he had seen me was at a point where my Danish was still 'getting there'. In what would prove to be a dress rehearsal for my departure from Denmark a month or so later, it came time to say my final farewell. I was close to tears, and holding them back was made all the more difficult by the fact that Josefine was openly sobbing. My host mother, too, had tears in her eyes. As the train pulled from the station, my tears finally beat me. I felt sad, not only for leaving, but for not having let my family see my tears. I was sure, though, that they knew how I felt.

About a week before Christmas, I visited with Michael's host family and several Rotarians from his club for Christmas lunch. It was a lovely lunch with celebrations extending well beyond the day and into the night. At one stage, the large candle in the centre of the table fell and the tablecloth caught alight. I made a dash from the kitchen to the table to extinguish it with the water that was already on the table. Despite the very late end to the evening, I was up very early. Clara and Bendt had invited me to spend the day with them, so I had to catch a bus home from Michael's, get showered and changed, then another two buses back out to Clara and Bendt's house.

Clara and Bendt invited me to take part in what had become an annual event for many of the residents living in their street. At 10:00am on Sunday, 20 December, a large group of residents from the street drove out of the city limits to a large pine tree forest heavily populated with trees of varying sizes. Each family walked around, found a suitable tree, cut it down and loaded it into their cars or onto their trailers. It seemed simple enough, perhaps even boring, but the Danes had an uncanny knack of making the ordinary, extraordinary. Once all the families had completed that activity, picnic tables were unloaded and we all sat around drinking coffee, tea and Gammel Dansk (liqueur bitters) and eating sandwiches, biscuits and cake. All the residents in my first host family's street knew each other and most were rather close friends. We returned with our tree, decorated it and joined with a number of other families for Christmas lunch, or as I then was able to call it, Jule Frokost. It was so enjoyable to participate in that day's activities, particularly when it meant so much to the people around me. The food was so varied with some traditional Danish Christmas fare that I had not previously tasted and the almost obligatory Christmas beer. Clara and Bendt really hosted a festive feast and we all went home with full stomachs and warm hearts.

Christmas Eve was spent with my last host family and it was so superbly special. The day was about traditions and observing them in the most enjoyable way. We woke early and immediately began toiling in the kitchen. In addition to preparing a scrumptious breakfast of cereal, hash-browns, breads and several varieties of fruit, we had to make some candy for the celebrations later that evening. We were all thankful for such abundance at breakfast and were reminded of the need to be thankful for life.

We walked about two kilometres to the nearby church and attended a Christmas service. It was the first Christmas service I had ever attended. As I sat through the service, I reflected on the good fortune I had enjoyed in being sent to Denmark and was thankful for that. While not particularly religious, it was hard not to be thankful in that setting. Of course, I was thankful for all the people that made exchange a reality for me, but also felt compelled to acknowledge that on some higher level, my 'Danish destiny' was scripted and directed to be the sensation that it was. Save for the odd disagreement when out at night and of course my Hamburg mishap, I had enjoyed an entire year of adventure, discovery, learning and personal growth. I had been unreservedly safe and secure throughout. I had visited safe places and some that required the exercise of caution. I had met many desirable people and a few that were not. I had challenged my palate to new sensations, some of which were delicious and some that were disgusting. I had been relaxed, but at other times completely exhausted to the point of delirium. I had experienced enormous and dizzying popularity and sometimes desperate and heartbreaking loneliness. I had enjoyed feelings of great success and achievement, but also frustration and failure. Of course, I had had a role to play in all of that, but I was thankful for having been raised as the person I was, able and willing to participate in the creation of the masterpiece that was my exchange. These reflections must have been on a deeper level and for longer than I was consciously aware, because before too long, the ninety-minute service drew to a close with what I understood to be the usual blessings.

Upon returning home, I was treated to a telephone call from my family in Australia. They, too, were celebrating Christmas away from home, in Sydney with my Grandmother. Hearing their voices at Christmas time reminded me how much I missed them, but I took enormous comfort from being with people I also truly loved.

Christmas Eve evening was as foreign to me as Denmark had been almost twelve months earlier. It was like nothing I had experienced before. I had danced many times before, but to do so with linked arms around a Christmas tree, together with a loving family, was an extraordinary experience that words fail to properly describe. The dancing, combined with singing by all, created a phenomenon I knew would be cherished forever. My last host family had elaborately decorated their home with Christmas ornaments and Danish flags. At dinner time, we all gathered in the large formal dining room, which was complete with chandeliers, a large solid timber table, piano and of course, the Christmas tree. Following a most heavenly dinner, the table was cleared to make way for numerous presents to be placed in the middle. Then I was introduced to yet another new custom – Jule Spil. It was a Christmas game where all those present at dinner placed gifts on the table then started rolling a dice. Each time a player rolled a six, he or she took a gift from the table and passed on the dice. The game was timed and this could be varied to personal preference. The game became particularly interesting when all gifts were taken from the table, then as the game continued, players took gifts from each other. Once the predetermined time had expired, each player kept the gifts they had collected. Christmas Eve 1992 was unquestionably the most unique and unforgettable Christmas I had ever experienced.

The days between Christmas and New Year were ever so busy. They were so busy that the one day I rested and relaxed was noteworthy for that reason alone. I still had friends to farewell for the last time and had family functions to attend.

I knew that I would be spending time in the city during my many farewells, so I had asked Mum and Dad to send me a boomerang and some brochures about Australia to give to Ingrid at the tourist bureau. I bundled them together and made my final visit to Ingrid to wish her an appreciative farewell and a merry Christmas. Her teary eyes suggested to me that perhaps I had impacted the lives of a number of Danes in much the same was as they had so positively impacted mine.

Just as Christmas Eve had been memorable, so too was New Year's Eve. In its own way, it was probably even bigger than Christmas Eve with more of a party atmosphere. It started very early for me as I had been visiting Matthew in Ry and had to make my return to Aarhus before anything else could be done. We spent the day setting up rocket launchers for our fireworks at midnight and finalising dinner. We had many people visit, which added to the excitement.

Each New Year's Eve, the Queen of Denmark would address her people in a television broadcast, and I was informed that nearly every Dane watches or listens to that address. At midnight, we watched a special countdown on the television, then ran outside to set off the fireworks that we had purchased earlier in the day. It was tremendously cold, but we all wore our coats, and most of us were smoking cigars. The fireworks display was spectacular. The residents in and around my host family's street all participated in an informal and friendly competition to see who had the most elaborate and extensive fireworks. Without doubt, ours won on that occasion. The fireworks competition was something they had been doing each year for many years. Our two rockets were a hit and were as substantial as any single fireworks explosion I had seen. As we stood there in that cold winter's night, we could hear all the neighbours yelling and clapping as we were for them. It remained for us to have our first meal for 1993, and we returned to the welcoming warmth of the house for that purpose. After enjoying our meal, I made a short and largely impromptu speech. I bid farewell to those of our guests that I wouldn't see again and made public my appreciation of my last host family and indeed all my families.

The realisation that I only had four days left in the country hit me at that time and hit me hard. I had just celebrated the beginning of a new year that I would share little of with those I had come to love dearly. The end to exchange is inevitable, and it served no useful purpose to try and reject that premise. I shed a tear or two, but the comfort of my host family was immediate, and I concluded on a positive note.

14

A Final Farewell

In this mortal world of ours, everything eventually ends. Sadly, in the case of youth exchange, it all started and finished in a year. I guess that could be stretched to two years if the selection process and briefing camps were included in the calculation. I guess further to that, in a desperate bid to defeat its 'end', it might be stretched to three years if participation in further briefing camps as a returned exchange student was also included. While the actual exchange may have started and ended in twelve months, the memories I was sure, would never end.

My good friend Michael had, some weeks earlier, held a farewell party that I attended. It was a raucous affair with a number of his friends from school and some members of his host families present. Given my many attendances at his school and in his host town, I was known to most of those at the party. I was staying at Michael's house that evening, which was just as well, because the party didn't end until about 3:00am. Despite the late hour at which I retired to the bedroom, I woke just before 9:00am the next day. It was difficult to remain asleep when an attractive girl was kissing me. Lena was one of Michael's friends whom I had met several times prior to that party. Lena was the last of Michael's guests to leave, besides myself of course. I remained with Michael to help clean up after the party and to share an exquisite lunch with his host mother. After lunch, his host mother presented me with a lovely gift and bid me a heartfelt goodbye. It was the first time I felt the sadness that was attached to her words. I had bid her farewell on many previous visits, but this was the last visit I was to make before leaving the country altogether. I was not assured of ever seeing her again and that was difficult for both of us.

I had no thoughts of a going-away party. I had so much planned for my final weeks in Denmark, and a party would have simply been too difficult to arrange. Importantly, though, my host families had already done more than enough for me throughout my exchange and, in my mind, a party wasn't necessary. My farewells were intensely personal, choosing instead to visit friends for a lunch here or a dinner there. Sometimes, it was little more than a couple of beers.

Apart from my host families, the goodbye I feared most was that with Hanne. Simply put, I didn't want to say goodbye. I must have picked up the telephone over ten times before I could bring myself to dial her number. I did, and we met later that day at a local pizza restaurant where we indulged in great food and beer before returning to her house. We looked at recent photographs I had taken, read through my yearbook and the Euro-Tour diary. We again watched some videos from home and listened to music. Most importantly I guess, we did that which only close friends can do. We laughed, we cried, we reflected on how we had become such good friends. Despite her beauty being of the highest order, Hanne and I had never allowed intimacy to infiltrate our relationship, which probably made it stronger. I certainly felt attracted to her in the romantic sense when we first met and, indeed, for some time later. I sensed though, that Hanne was a rare and precious soul, and I didn't want either of us to reflect in the years ahead with the slightest regret. This was often the risk at the end of physical relationships, and it wasn't a risk I was prepared to take. The day turned into night and I had to return home. We gave each other heartfelt assurances of always keeping in touch and a hug that I wished would be eternal. It wasn't and as I kissed her cheek,

I said goodbye to my dearest friend in Denmark. The sky was dark, but not nearly as dark as the feeling in my heart as I walked toward the bus stop. The realisation hit me that I had no idea when I was going to see Hanne again. My bus arrived, but I didn't board it. I was, by that stage, struggling with reality and was sobbing uncontrollably. The next bus arrived about fifteen minutes later, which was about the same amount of time it took me to compose myself.

Leaving Australia had been very difficult for me. Leaving Denmark was far harder. It was strong testament to the success of any exchange if bidding farewell was hard to do. The harder it was, the better the exchange. The justification for this assertion was simple and based largely on the bonds forged with family and friends. I had grown to love all there was about Denmark, but mostly I had discovered the love, respect and admiration of people on a level reserved only for my natural parents and sisters. Those people were my host parents and host brothers and sisters. Similarly, the friendships made were strong. They were also unique in the sense that their life-long characteristic had been achieved not in a lifetime, but in a year.

When I departed Australia, I knew that in a year's time, I would return home. My ticket for that purpose had long before been booked. In that fact was a degree of comfort as I embarked upon my journey. However, there was no such return ticket booked to Denmark and no indication at all as to when I might return. In my travels, I had met Rotarians who told me that there were some exchange students that they had never heard from again, let alone saw again. That frightened me, but also inspired me to promise that I would not be one of those students.

Another reason leaving Denmark was far harder was the doubt I harboured about 'life' once home. I wondered what my existing relationships would be like, given that a part of me had forevermore become Danish. I wondered what my future relationships might be like – would they, or could they, measure up to those I had enjoyed in Denmark. I was fearful that my 'normal' life might not be able to deliver the stimulation that came with the new experiences, the new discoveries and the new learnings that I had enjoyed on an almost daily basis in Denmark. As a consequence of those types of thoughts came the realisation of a truly bizarre phenomenon. Almost twelve months earlier, I left Australia not knowing what to expect of my life in Denmark. There I was, as the countdown toward my return continued, not knowing what to expect of my life in Australia.

The quality of my sleep on the eve of my departure was poor. My nerves, excitement and anticipation couldn't be ignored and I woke many times throughout the night. The morning, despite being cold, was delightful. The sun was shining in all its glory and was melting what was only the faintest covering of frost on the lawns. I thought at the time that perhaps I was meant to always remember the beauty of Denmark as it was that morning. It was beautiful and was worth remembering. In true Danish fashion, however, the weather changed dramatically as my afternoon departure approached. The contrast was frightening. In fact, it was historic.

Within a matter of hours, the entire district was frozen. It wasn't a snowstorm or some raging blizzard – it was worse. It was one of the many wonders of nature that occur without warning and largely without explanation. Newspapers reported it as the worst ice storm in forty years. Motor vehicles were colliding or skidding off roads, elderly pedestrians were falling and injuring themselves, and the emergency services were working on full alert.

We hadn't been notified of any cancellation or delay, so my host family decided we should still venture out to the airport to see whether my flight would be leaving, delayed or cancelled altogether. Aage, returning home from work, couldn't drive up our street due to the slippery conditions, so Agnes, Victor and I set off by foot to meet him at the main road. We wrapped my suitcase in a plastic bag and simply slid it along beside us. The ground was just that slippery. It was a very slow drive to the airport and perhaps the perfect example of why allowing for contingencies was always important on exchange. Susan, the other Australian on exchange in Aarhus, had also managed to safely arrive at the airport. Given the worsening conditions, we were informed that our flight was, in fact, cancelled and we were rebooked on an alternative flight the following afternoon.

It was such a devastating anti-climax. I had summoned the courage to say goodbye but hadn't needed to. I wasn't at all sure how to feel or how to react. Part of preparing emotionally to say goodbye had been to focus on the excitement of seeing my family and friends at home. That too, was delayed. I was disappointed on two levels, which thrust me into a temporary state of melancholy. I had been disappointed about my impending departure for some time, but also disappointed that I didn't leave as planned. As had often been the solution, I focused on the positive. I had been blessed with one further day in Denmark and was not going to wallow in sadness at being there.

My last night in Denmark saw me suffer a serious case of déjà vu. My feelings of having previously experienced that same situation were not illusory, but very real. They were no easier the second time around and I retired to bed for another restless night.

There was no stopping me the next day. The weather again started fine and remained that way, at least until after I left. As I had done the day before, I met Susan and together we checked in our luggage and obtained our boarding passes. The call came for us to board and we bid farewell to our respective host families. I felt the tears welling in my eyes but managed to win the fight to hold them back. I wanted to leave on a positive note with an appreciative and loving smile for my host family to remember me by. Sitting on the plane just prior to take-off was a soul-searching experience for me. It was the realisation that my exchange was at an end and the discovery that I had changed, learned and loved so very much in such a short time.

Susan and I arrived in Copenhagen without further incident. We joined about fifteen other students who had also been delayed by the inclement conditions and boarded our international flight to Singapore. It came as a great surprise therefore, when we saw on the television screen that our destination was Bangkok. After the initial scare, we were assured all was in order and we would ultimately arrive in Singapore. The one most recurrent theme of exchange was that the experiences never end. In my quiet moment of solitude aboard the plane from Aarhus to Copenhagen, I thought my exchange was over, leaving only the mere formality of returning home. I was wrong. We did arrive in Bangkok but did not leave as expected. It was a national holiday and an air show was being held at the airport. As a result, we had a further delay of more than an hour before we could take-off. That delay had its own unfortunate consequences, because once we arrived in Singapore, I discovered that I had missed my Qantas flight to Brisbane. A number of other students had also missed connecting flights to other parts of Australia and were treated to five-star hotel accommodation. I was given the option of joining the other students overnight in Singapore or being re-booked on a Singapore Airlines flight. Given I had already been delayed for more than a day, I chose the latter and left Singapore within an hour or so of my arrival.

That flight represented the most difficult eight hours of my life. While it was a relatively full flight, I was very much alone. Every flight I had taken on exchange had been with other students and in some cases, Rotarians. My much-cherished Rotary jacket, a striking memento of exchange, was the topic of much conversation with a number of people on the flight. It helped time pass, although eventually most went to sleep. I was extremely tired, having had two restless nights before my departure, but still could not sleep. I had even taken one of my host father's sleeping tablets upon leaving Singapore but to no avail. By that stage, the pure excitement of seeing my family and friends again was so overwhelming. My inability to fall asleep was frustrating, because I couldn't escape the expectation and excitement.

As difficult as it was, time did pass. It had passed every day of the year I was away and I figured that it had to pass while in flight. Eventually, we began our descent to Brisbane and the moment the plane landed I lost the brave face. The emotion of it all had been threatening to consume me all the way from Aarhus and with the landing, it succeeded. I sobbed but did so quite proudly upon reflection of what I'd just done. When I embarked on exchange, I had taken with me a passion for ideas, a hunger for learning and an insatiable desire for exploration and discovery. I sat content in the knowledge that I had been exposed to so many different ideas, about so many different things. There was no doubt in my mind that my hunger for learning had been fed and my desire to explore had been exceeded. I had held absolutely nothing back as I embraced the exchange experience.

I was overjoyed though, when the fasten seatbelt signs were disengaged. I hurriedly regained my composure and disembarked the aircraft. Upon entering the airport, I began to think that I would never finish the return journey as Customs was extremely busy. I had declared some items, such as the last uneaten rye bread sandwich my host mother had made for me to take on the flight. Despite my plea to eat it immediately, it was taken. I had in my possession, slightly more alcohol than permitted, but that was overlooked in consideration of the seizure of my cherished Danish delicacy.

I ventured into the arrivals area of the airport and was immediately swamped by my ever-loving mother. Her flow of joyous tears was clear evidence that she was quite overcome at finally having her son home. I had time enough to briefly greet my father and sisters before a rowdy crowd of friends, less overcome by my return, but most certainly happy about it, jumped all over me in a hearty welcome home gesture. We drove home from Brisbane, stopping only to enjoy my first real meat pie in over a year. Home felt so very good, as did the company of my family and friends.

Because of the delays I had experienced with my flights, the day of my arrival was also the date for my surprise welcome home party. That was a story unto itself. It was abundantly obvious to me that my good friends were just as close to me as the day I had left, and for that, I was most thankful. I knew that returning from such an experience was going to be difficult, but with my family and friends by my side, I was confident I would cope.

On the 8th of January 1993, I penned the final words in my exchange diary and closed the book. I knew, however, that while the book may have closed, the story would forever be open and continue to live in my heart and my mind.

Epilogue

The story has now been told – it needed to be. It will never be read with the same passion with which it was lived, but it's in the telling, not the reading, that the purpose is served. The confidence I held at the end of my exchange that the memories would survive the passing of time, was not misplaced. Those memories remain, and remain vividly. The love I have for my host families has not waned, nor theirs for me and the true and dear friendships continue to this day. I am still very much a part of their lives, as they are a part of mine.

More than 30 years have passed since exchange and Rotary Youth Exchange is still very much a significant part of who I am. It's no longer something that I 'do', or did, but is something that I 'am'. I have, since my exchange, become a Rotarian and was a club and district counsellor to exchange students. The continued involvement with Rotary has seen my fondness for the organisation grow. It has seen me expand my sphere of involvement from only youth exchange to other very worthwhile and effective Rotary programs for youth.

My family has enjoyed hosting over 25 exchange students, which creates for all of us an entirely new range of exchange experiences. It also inspired my youngest daughter to become an exchange student to Italy in 2019. She now understands the profound impact of exchange and has a greater understanding of my journey. Importantly, she, too, has close bonds with her host families and to Rotary. She has her own stories to share and memories to hold dear.

Significantly, I have continued on my journey of becoming Danish. I have introduced my family to Denmark, to my host families and to my friends in Denmark. They too, have enjoyed the sights, the sounds, the foods. They have experienced the extraordinary love and generosity of my host families, who welcomed us all into their homes. My links with Denmark remain as strong as ever, if not stronger in many ways. I have hosted students from Denmark in my home and with that, have widened my circle of Danish family. Almost a decade after exchange, my then wife and I enjoyed the company of, and personal introduction to, the then Royal Highness, Crown Prince Frederik and Her Royal Highness, Crown Princess Mary of Denmark at a Royal cocktail party in Sydney.

I have on my life's continuing journey, read many books and attended seminars with a friend of mine who subscribes to the messages contained within them. I have read and heard how in life, business or almost any endeavour, it's wise to identify other successful people and 'model' yourself on their performance. My view, though, is that if we all look like or behave like others, how do we differentiate ourselves as being unique. How can we be better, if we look or behave the same.

Exchange in Denmark taught me that different is good, to stand out is to be recognised. To be recognised is to discover opportunity and to embrace opportunity is to succeed. Because the measure of success is different to all of us, so too must be the journey to achieve that success.

In telling this story, it is my hope that it provides a more profound appreciation of the life-changing nature of youth exchange. I also hope it provides an insight into Denmark and its people, because it is a tremendously special place, populated as it is with tremendously special people.

There will forever be a part of me that is Danish.

www.ingramcontent.com/pod-product-compliance
Lightning Source LLC
Chambersburg PA
CBHW060600080526
44585CB00013B/629